The Power of Your Attitudes

● LESLIE PARROTT ●

The
POWER
of Your
ATTITUDES

BEACON HILL PRESS OF KANSAS CITY
Kansas City, Missouri

First Printing, 1967

ISBN: 083-410-1513

Printed in the
United States of America

Preface

In a cozy beach-house one hundred yards from the Pacific Ocean and within hearing of its rhythms, the problems of life can seem quite remote. But back home where most of the living is done, both Christ and the concrete city are very real. The difference between here and home is like the difference between the classroom and Main Street, between camp meeting and back on the job, between Sunday night services and Monday morning schedules. Everyone needs days away, time in the classroom, the spiritual refurbishing of camp meeting, and the religious help of a Sunday night service. But most of life is lived under the pressures of the roaring city, the contradictions of Main Street, the demands back on the job, and the pressure of insistent daily schedules. The idyllic existence of an unstructured life on a South Pacific isle is for scripts. Real life is lived where the people are, where the problems come in all sizes, and without end.

The variables which determine the effectiveness of sidestepping, alleviating, or tackling these problems of life are many, but none is more important than the power of a right attitude; and the power of a right attitude depends on the presence and person of Jesus Christ. To the power of this attitude and the presence of this Person, this little volume is dedicated with the prayer and the hope that it may be helpful.

An honest debt is due three men: Mr. Elden Rawlings, who first suggested the need for this material; Dr. W. T. Purkiser, who gave encouragement and authorization for reprinting some of these pieces which first appeared in the *Herald of Holiness;* and Mr. Bud Lunn, whose persistence resulted in the final manuscript.

—LESLIE PARROTT

Contents

The Power of Your Attitudes

It is no accident that some people are beaten down, defeated, and anxiety-ridden while other people are productive, effective, and useful. It is no accident that some people take problems and trials in stride and rise above them while other persons who seemingly have as much concern for spiritual things are disoriented by the least irregularity. It is no accident that some people are in charge of their work and on schedule while other people are always being pushed by their work and generally are snowed under. The reason these contrasts in people are no accident is that they are the result of the attitudes of these different people.

The person who goes against the laws of physical science does not break them but is broken by them. For instance, the man who jumps from the tall building does not break the law of gravity; it breaks him. Ignorance of these laws affords no indulgence; when they are broken, the breaker suffers. And just as there are laws in the physical world, there are also the inexorable laws of God which relate to the mind. Whether these laws are known or correctly understood is not the issue; they are operative and when broken the person involved suffers. Wrong attitudes of the mind can produce ugly facial lines, break homes, create psychosomatic illnesses in endless variety, deteriorate friendships, disorganize work habits, and even cause an early death. A constructive set of attitudes, on the other hand, can result in a face which reflects character and kindness, a happy, united family, good mental health, physical well-being, lasting friendships, productive work habits, and a more fulfilled life. The determining factor is the power of your attitudes. At least four contrasting types of attitudes have enormous leverage in the fulcrum of human fulfillment or destruction:

First are the attitudes of *love and resentment*. Identical experiences result in greater love and understanding in one person while producing the creeping paralysis of bitterness and resentment in another, and in both instances the attitude was a matter of choice. No person who has lived to adult years is free from a history of events which might have justified resentment and bitterness had this been his choice. But the man who chooses the attitude of love becomes more useful and productive while the one who chooses to be bitter is forging more bars for his own self-made prison of eventual isolation.

Second are the attitudes of *courage and self-pity*. Two deaths in a single auto accident leave two widows to face life alone. One becomes courageous, strikes out to make a life for herself, and actually enters a whole new era which has its own kinds of rewards and experiences. The other widow chooses to feel sorry for herself and in spite of the reassurances from friends becomes more retiring, complains more, develops physical symptoms, and in general sets in motion the attitudes which complicate her own existence.

Third are the attitudes of *deceit and honesty*. Sin (which always is some form of deceit) wrecks marriage, makes hyocrites of well-meaning people, and lowers self-esteem. Grace and forgiveness make for honesty which is candid instead of posed, real instead of assumed, genuine instead of synthetic. And it is within the power of each person to choose the continuing regard for genuine transparent honesty, instead of the tangled strands of a hopelessly confused life which results when one follows the road of deceit.

Fourth are the attitudes of *positive and negative perspective* of life. Every person takes the sum total of all the experiences in life and puts them together in a pattern which is either positive or negative. He sees the things which happen to him as falling in pleasant places or as the work of designing people who have intended to hurt him. Two men lose their jobs. One sees this as the end of the world and another as the dawn of a new day. One man sees the loss of the job as the result of a plot of evil men while the other sees it as the providence of God.

Dr. Victor Frankl, who stood under the glaring lights of a Gestapo court in a Nazi concentration camp, said that the black-booted soldiers had taken from him every earthly possession—clothes, watch, even his wedding ring. He stood there naked, his body shaved. He was destitute but for one thing. They had taken from him all that he had except the power to choose his own attitude. This they could not touch.

The Worst Kind of Cancer

Cancer may do its evil work in the lungs, throat, brain, bone marrow, or any other part of the body—even the skin. But the worst kind of cancer isn't in the body tissues at all. It works its devastation in the place where the real self dwells. This cancer is resentment.

Resentment starts small, and grows almost imperceptibly at first. It may smolder like volcanic fire in the heart of the earth or gallop through the system like rivers of hot lava. But the results are the same. Unless the victim responds to radical treatment, the force of life is soon spent.

Resentment may begin with a social rebuff, a flash of jealousy, a chance remark, a certain look on someone's face, or no look at all. But from these tiny virus infections resentment takes root. The object of resentment may be a member of the household, a colleague, a classmate, the pastor, a church leader, or even a fellow pastor. It could be a child. But in any case the results are there. Resentment causes a breakdown in communications, lines in people's faces ahead of their years, the development of impossible human-relations problems, and the increase of all kinds of psychosomatic symptoms from aches and pains to rashes and tics.

A girl in a Nazarene College had a life history of resentment toward her dad. The cancer of her resentment grew until it covered the church, the college, her husband, and almost anyone with whom she was associated for any length of time. But in a pastor's study the radical surgery of the Holy Spirit eradicated resentment and set her free for useful, happy living. At the last report she dated the beginning of "real living" from the day God cured the cancer of resentment.

There is a clear-cut remedy for resentment; but it isn't easy.

1. Become aware of resentment and accept it for what it is. People who have become accustomed to giving pat answers to problems of attitude aften find it difficult to see resentment in themselves. People who tend toward feelings of religious superiority such as self-righteousness and legalism diagnose resentment in others more quickly than in themselves.

2. Be willing to give up resentment. This isn't always easy. Resentment becomes a psychological crutch for support in personal failure. Since the object of resentment becomes the excuse for life's failures, people do not move readily toward giving up their crutch. For when the crutch is gone, the person has to choose between falling flat or standing on his own feet of personal responsibility.

3. Work diligently at seeing things from the viewpoint of the person or persons who are the immediate occasion of the resentment. This, too, is difficult. Most people have spent a lifetime interpreting all they see and hear from their own slant. Seeing and feeling things through the eyes and emotions of another does not change facts but it does help alleviate the pain.

4. Depend on the grace of God through the Holy Spirit literally to remove the last vestige of the cancerous resentment. The Great Physician not only can cure. He will. And He does. He performs the spiritual surgery and heals the wound with the balm of Christian love and understanding.

The Therapy of God

Since the days of Sigmund Freud in Europe and William James in America, the developing branches of psychology have been striving to diagnose more accurately the ills of men's minds. Among the many tools now used are standardized tests, projective techniques, free association, and nondirective counseling. Even the man on Main Street has learned to identify mental disturbances by name. He knows that "neurotic," "psychotic," "paranoid," and "hypochondriac" are terms used to describe people who have crippling worries, deteriorated personalities, exaggerated fears, and imaginary illnesses.

The strength of modern psychology is its capacity to diagnose. But once the diagnosis is made, the wide road of understanding narrows into a dead end of frustration and disappointment for most seekers of help. Psychotherapy stretches over long periods of weekly visits. Expense is great. The nomenclature is strange. A great amount of faith in the therapist is demanded of the patient. The entire process is often a threat. For a few there is immediate relief by prescription; for most, the therapy is disappointing. But for the ministers and laymen who have enough human understanding to recognize the symptoms and enough grace to overcome feelings

14

of rejection, the troubled person may be offered the most potent therapy on earth—the therapy of God. "I am come," Jesus said, "that they might have life, and that they might have it more abundantly" (John 10:10).

1. The therapy of God begins with forgiveness. An eminent psychiatrist was lecturing to a group of West Coast ministers, and not knowing a Nazarene was in the group, said, "I know of only one Protestant denomination which majors on confession and forgiveness, and that is the Church of the Nazarene. They have an altar where people are urged to confess their sins and pray to God for forgiveness in the presence of the pastor and a small group from the congregation." Self-incriminating behavior, which results in guilt, can be alleviated by one cure only, the forgiveness of God.

2. The therapy of God includes cleansing. Behavior which originates in a depraved mind must be forgiven. But the depraved condition itself is subject only to the cleansing of the atonement. If the power of Christ is equal to the challenge of forgiveness but not cleansing, then it is only half a cure. It is the cleansing which makes possible the life of love. This, indeed, is the mind of Christ in you.

3. The therapy of God includes restitution. This old-fashioned word, which was once ignored by so many, is now coming into a newfound status. The man who has been forgiven and cleansed seeks further peace through reconciliation with his neighbor.

4. Last, the therapy of God includes the inner strength of His presence. The Christian religion is not built on an ironclad theology or accurately stated creeds, but on the person of Jesus Christ. His inner presence assures the transformed man the continuity of a wholesome, useful life even beyond death. "I live; yet not I, but Christ liveth in me . . . I can do all things through Christ which strengtheneth me."

The Problem of Human Suffering

(PART ONE)

The lady fairly shouted in anger and heartbreak: "We thought God would care for us. We've gone to church and Sunday school, paid our tithe, had family devotions and everything . . . and now God let my husband get killed. Tell me why."

In the same afternoon of visitation, another lady pointed through her window to a house across the street, all the time talking petulantly: "See that house! That man is so wicked and vile we sometimes call the children in to keep them from hearing his outrages. He never goes to church! He makes fun of churches, and preachers, and us. He works in the same place my husband works, and my husband got laid off and that man kept his job. Now tell me why. Why is it we suffer and he gloats?"

The problem of suffering is as old as one of the most ancient pieces of sacred or secular literature, the Book of Job. All forty-two chapters deal with the problem of why a good man suffers. In the New Testament, the great "Hall of Faith" (Hebrews 11) outlines the impressive achievements of great men and women whose faith has earned them special mention: Enoch, Noah, Abraham, Isaac, Jacob, Joseph, Moses, and many of

16

which "time would fail me to tell." But the pivot in this account is the little phrase, "and others." These "others" who had a "good report through faith, received not the promise." They also had faith; but for it they "had trial of cruel mockings and scourgings, yea, moreover of bonds and imprisonment." Even Jesus did not escape. In the last moments of His life He agonized, "My God, my God, why hast thou forsaken me?" Stripped of its qualifying words, this cry may be reduced to two words, "Why Me?"

But what do we know about suffering? First, it is not an illusion. To say, "Oh, she's really not sick! It's only in her head," is unfair. Psychosomatic pain is as real as any other kind. The headache may be caused by an imaginary fear but the pain is nonetheless real.

Further, suffering is not necessarily caused by the sins of the sufferer. Job, through the worst kind of torment, was convinced of this. He continued to affirm, "I know that my redeemer liveth." Jesus hit this idea of sin and suffering among those "that told him of the Galilaeans, whose blood Pilate had mingled with their sacrifices" (Luke 13:1). Knowing their minds, Jesus said, "Suppose ye that these Galilaeans were sinners above all the Galilaeans, because they suffered these things?" His resounding answer was, "I tell you, Nay." Continuing to teach that suffering does not necessarily come because of the sins of the sufferer, He said, "Or those eighteen, upon whom the tower in Siloam fell, and slew them, think ye that they were sinners above all men that dwelt in Jerusalem? I tell you, Nay." And concerning the man who was born blind, Jesus said, "Neither hath this man sinned, nor his parents" (John 9:3). Sin causes suffering, but not all suffering is caused by the sins of the sufferer.

Also, it is a mistake to blame suffering on God. Trouble often comes into the lives of those who reject God, but it also comes into the lives of those who walk with Him. The rain falls on the just and on the unjust, and the drought is likewise no respecter of persons.

The problem of human suffering is universal but it is not simple. There are no easy answers. But we can be sure on the basis of Scripture and human experience that (1) suffering is not an illusion, (2) it is not necessarily the result of sins committed, and (3) it is wrong to blame God. Why then do good people suffer? This question will be answered in the next step.

Why Do Good People Suffer?

(PART TWO)

Suffering is not an illusion! Also, it is not necessarily the result of sins committed by the sufferer. Sins bring suffering, but not all suffering is the immediate result of sin. And James further suggests that tribulations do not come from God. "God cannot be tempted . . . neither tempteth he any man" (Jas. 1:13). Why, then, do good people suffer? Only God knows the final answer. But there are some rather certain reasons why good people are not immune to suffering:

First, good people suffer whenever they break the laws of God. What some have called "the inexorable laws of God" operate in both the physical world and in the minds and hearts of men—in nature and in human nature. If a good man breaks the law of gravity he suffers, regardless of his state of grace. In fact the law is not broken; it remains. It is the person who is broken when he goes against the law of gravity. Likewise a person who is correct theologically will suffer if he breaks God's laws about love and forgiveness. In fact all kinds of pains have developed in people who have broken the eleventh commandment: "A new commandment I give unto you, That ye love one another; as I have loved you" (John 13:34).

Homes have been divided, people's faces have become lined ahead of their years, and psychosomatic ailments of many kinds have resulted when God's laws on such matters as love, faith, optimism, and Christian usefulness have been ignored. These laws of human nature and the kinds of suffering they produce are just as real as the laws of physics concerning moving objects —and good people are subject to both.

Second, good people suffer because of the interdependence of the human race. The breakfast coffee served today came through many hands of many people in a variety of vocations in several lands before it finally was poured into a cup by the side of your plate. But this same interdependence which brings unending blessings also has its liabilities. The armed forces assure our continued freedoms but take the sons we love to make this possible. The high-powered automobile and the superhighway which bring us great joy in rapid transportation also may be the place and occasion for extreme physical suffering and perhaps a prelude to death. If we accept the blessing of jet aviation we also accept the liability of possible suffering and death because of interdependence on others. "As by one man sin entered into the world," so by one man's miscalculations can death and destruction come to many. We live in a constant state of interdependence with others.

Third, good people suffer because God, in His sovereign will, created an orderly world of cause and effect. Therefore it rains on the just and on the unjust.

And winds of tornado or hurricane force destroy the brothel as well as the church, the Christian college as well as the secular university. Cancer-causing viruses may just as likely do their deadly work in the body of the saint as in that of the gangster.

Last, suffering is a part of life. Each person in his own time and way is subjected to his share of grief. The really important question is not why it has come to us, but how we will choose to react to the suffering which is our share in life. We have only three options:

1. We may resent suffering and therefore waste time and energy in bitter blaming and second guessing.

2. We may accept suffering stoically and trudge on through life wearily bearing our burdens.

3. Or we may learn how to grow and mature through suffering. A voice coach said of a brilliant singer who performed with precision and power that she never could be a really great singer because she had never suffered. Suffering taken in the right attitude is therapeutic. It makes for growth and development. For "we know that all things [are made to] work together for good to them that love God . . . If God be for us, who can be against us?" (Rom. 8:28-31)

Temptations to Good People

While mature saints testify with glowing assurance about continuing victory, beginning Christians may think they got that way because the hound dogs of temptation have left them alone. However, the Bible indicates temptation is a lifelong problem. "Watch and pray, that ye enter not into temptation" (Matt. 26:41), was not said to confirmed sinners but to the three closest followers of Jesus (Peter, James, and John), and just after they had left an inspiring service in the Upper Room. The Apostle Paul included himself as a prospect for temptation when he said, "Lest Satan should get an advantage of us: for we are not ignorant of his devices" (II Cor. 2:11).

Only the nature of temptation changes; temptation itself is always present either latent or active. Christians may resist or cooperate but the evil presence of the devil is always at the door with a new and more subtly attractive offer in exchange for Christian influence and or inner soul peace. To good people who have matured beyond the devil's power to direct them into fleshly sins, there are three crafty temptations which Satan uses with devastating effectiveness.

1. The devil tempts good people on the matter of *feelings*. Three tested and tried accusations are made against sensitive Christians: (*a*) He says, "You don't feel right." Most people could agree with this at some time on most any given day. If "feeling right" is a

combination of physical well-being, good mental health, and spiritual sensitivity, then most people find the interaction of these three factors is not constant. (b) With increased leverage Satan snarls, "You don't feel as you formerly felt." Since life is a succession of emotional hills and valleys, this accusation is always true. (c) And as a final dig he observes rightly, "You don't feel as other people claim they feel." This also is true, for no two people are built on the same emotional pattern.

2. The devil tempts good people on the matter of *spiritual pride*. The strongest language Jesus ever used was against the Pharisees. He called them hypocrites! And their major sin was spiritual pride. They were proud of the strict way they kept the law (such as Sabbath keeping and hand washing). They were proud of the way they dressed (long robes with sackcloth and ashes for special occasions). They were proud of their ability to pray (desiring to pray standing in the marketplaces). They were proud of their record of giving (preferring to have trumpets blown when they passed out alms). Jesus, like thinking people today, saw this brand of religious pride as a shoddy substitute for a deep devotional relationship with God.

3. The devil tempts good people on the matter of *impatience with others*. It is a mistaken idea that piety is proved by a severe attitude toward evildoers. Like doctors who fight disease but not the patient, Christians loathe sin but accept the sinner. It takes only an instant for a sinner to be transformed, but it takes years to grow oak-like spiritual giants. The new birth is instantaneous but the new orientation of life takes time to develop. When Christians are impatient with teenagers, new Christians, or Christians from different cultural backgrounds, they will be wise to recognize the symptom as part of Satan's most subtle temptation to good people.

22

How to Handle Criticism

Criticism is a part of life. The person who takes a step forward or stands to his feet or lifts his voice is subject to criticism. Even the man who never stands up or speaks out or takes a daring step cannot be promised immunity from criticism.

A team of sociologists interviewed every resident in a mill town in New England. Among other things they learned that each person admitted criticizing other men and women in the community. But each person was scandalized to learn he was in turn criticized by others. This double standard is universal. People pass quick opinions on what other persons do or say, but the same people are shocked to learn they have become the butt of somebody else's criticism.

One thing which makes criticism hurt is the grain of truth it often contains. Criticism grows out of negative feelings one person has toward another. A foible is lifted from the behavior and exaggerated beyond its true significance. It is like the engineer pulling the train past the station. It is the smattering of truth or half-truth overstated in the criticism which makes it hurt.

Even the perfect motives of Jesus often were misunderstood, resulting in malicious criticism. For a Bible exercise, read the four Gospels making a list of all the criticisms made against the Saviour. For instance: (a) They called Jesus a glutton (Matt. 11:19; Luke 7:34). (b) They called Him a winebibber (Matt. 11:19; Luke 7:34). (c) They criticized Jesus for His association with sinners (Matt. 9:11; Mark 2:16; Luke 5:30). (d) And

23

worst of all (from their point of view), they called Him a Samaritan (John 8:48). To say this last was like accusing a man of selling out to the enemy. But much more important to us than the criticisms made against Jesus are the exemplary ways He used to handle them:

1. Jesus saw no profit in wasting energy to fight criticism. After a long, hard day Jesus sent His disciples into a village to arrange food and lodging for the night. When the villagers refused hospitality to Jesus, the disciples became angry and wished to fight back by calling "fire to come down from heaven, and consume them" (Luke 9:54). But Jesus quietly reproved the disciples and went down the road to the next village, where they found food and lodging without incident. Productive energy can be frittered away in useless fighting of criticism.

2. Jesus handled criticism through human understanding (empathy). When His accusers maligned Him on the Cross with their accusations and mocking laughter, Jesus responded with a prayer which was divine: "Father, forgive them; for they know not what they do" (Luke 23:34). This might be paraphrased, "Father, forgive them, for they simply do not understand the issues that are involved." If we could structure the situation as our criticizers do, we could understand why they feel as they do, but this takes more inner spiritual strength than most people have.

3. Last, Jesus responded to criticism with an invitation to fellowship and acceptance. His accusers said, "Behold a man gluttonous, and a winebibber, a friend of publicans and sinners. . . . [Jesus answered], Come unto me, all ye that labour and are heavy laden, and I will give you rest" (Matt. 11:19, 28). There is only one Christian answer to criticism—love! This is not a sentimental, gushy love, but a deep, abiding attitude of acceptance and an extended hand of fellowship toward those who criticize.

24

Observations on Resentment

The insides of a cat were being watched through a fluoroscope in the laboratory. As the professor put it in laymen's language, "This cat's inside machinery was running like a sewing machine." The food was being taken in, deposited in the stomach, and progressing in keeping with the digestive processes of cats.

Then! The door was opened and the experimenter brought into the room a dog which the cat was known to dislike. The effect outwardly was immediately apparent. The cat's back began to bow. His fur rose. His eyes dilated.

Something began happening on the inside, too. The digestive processes began slowing down and finally they stopped altogether. The professor turned in dead seriousness to the class, "If resentment does that to cats, what do you think it does to human beings?"

Resentment *does* work like that. Everything goes along fine until resentment develops, and suddenly everything grinds to a halt. Most people who harbor resentment do not understand the price they pay for their feelings. Friendships are broken. Jobs are lost. Homes are demoralized. Psychosomatic illnesses develop. Personality grows brittle and unbending. Resilience and flexibility are lost from the personality. Emotions become unstable. Energies, which might have been turned outward in productive pursuits, are turned inward and

25

productivity drops; effectiveness dwindles. All of this comes from resentment. It is the worst disease of the mind.

Many persons tenaciously cling to their resentments because they feel they are justified in holding them. But justified or not, no person who wants to live a productive, happy life can afford to hold resentment. No person in the Bible was more justified in harboring resentment than was Joseph. He could have fought back, perhaps just sulked in self-pity, or floundered in the use of other ineffective defense mechanisms. But he did the only thing any strong man does—he rose above the persons and the places which might have provoked resentment within him. His brothers had rejected him. His boss's wife had lied about him, and the butler who promised to remember him didn't. Further, he wasted some precious time of his youth in a prison, serving time unjustly.

What are the preventive measures against resentment? Or what is the cure if resentment already has made its inroads in a person's mind? Here are three observations:

1. Become aware of the causes for resentment. There is usually not one but several causes for resentment. Resentment is a form of anger which grows out of jealousy, feelings of hostility, and feelings of frustration at our own inadequacies during the time of injustice. In Joseph's case he was first of all a rejected teen-ager. At seventeen he was sold by his brothers. He was handed a severe injustice in the lie told against him by Potiphar's wife. He was forgotten by a good friend whom he had helped. And last, he was frustrated by confinement in jail at a time when the thrust of life is at its strongest.

2. Resentment which begins with a specific experience can become diffused and spread out to tarnish

26

everything life touches. Life is not lived in compartments. People who are resentful in one part of life will either handle the resentment immediately or it will spread into other areas of life. Resentment that crops up on the job, in the home, at church, or in social relationships will soon spread like gangrene to all areas of life.

3. Resentment can be cured only by your own willingness to receive the cleansing of the Holy Spirit. A person may rationalize his problem of resentment by believing his feelings are justified because of the injustice he has suffered. He may further excuse himself on the grounds that resentment is a problem everybody faces. This does not change the fact. Resentment is a sin. And there is no adequate solution for sin except forgiveness and cleansing.

What Is a Sibling, Anyhow?

Several years ago the schools of Kansas City sent home brief questionnaires to be answered by parents. There were only three or four questions, but one of them was this: "Does this child have any siblings?" Angry parents wrote back sarcastic replies. The more irate wrote letters to the editors of the local papers while others kept the switchboard blinking at the superintendent's office. In a hundred different ways they all asked the same question, "What is a sibling, anyhow?"

Sibling is a convenient term used more often by psychologists and children's workers to refer to the brothers and sisters of a child. It is a kind of psychological shorthand like the word spouse used on many questionnaire forms to refer to a married person's husband or wife. But whether or not we use the term sibling, every family knows the problems of brothers and sisters getting along with each other.

There is a traditional belief dating back to the story of Cain and Abel, and formalized by Psychologist Alfred Adler, that there necessarily exists among siblings a spirit of competition, jealousy, and hostility. An older child, for instance, may feel that a new baby has deposed him from his reigning position in his parents' affections. A younger sibling, on the other hand, may envy his older brother's or sister's size, strength, and privileges. If these feelings of competition are not minimized, they can become fixed and persist throughout the life of the family, even into adulthood and old age. Sibling rivalry brings its harvest of discord and argument with increased rivalry and hurt feelings.

What are the things parents may do to reduce family friction among children? Here are a few suggestions:

1. Parents, premeditatedly, can prove they are impartial. This is a difficult line to walk: each child must be recognized and loved as a child who is different from the others. At the same time all the children must be treated alike with fairness and impartiality. Rivalry and discord are greatly increased if the children sense that one among them is a favorite with one or both parents or grandparents. Joseph's coat is a continuing symbol of parental preference and its result. It seems Jacob would have learned an eternal lesson on favoritism by seeing the lifetime wedge driven between him and Esau. But in his own home Jacob made the same error by acknowledging to the rest of his sons that Joseph had a special place in his heart. As a result, Joseph was sold into slavery, Jacob's heart was broken, and the

brothers—having lied to cover their first sin—spent the rest of their days in fear and guilt. Even after the family was united in Egypt, the scars of sin which began as sibling rivalry did not heal. "And when Joseph's brethren saw that their father was dead, they said, Joseph will peradventure hate us, and will certainly requite us all the evil which we did unto him" (Gen. 50:15).

2. Another antidote to rivalry and discord among children is the practice of Christian consistency by parents. Admiring my friend who had raised five children who were all in the church as pastors, pastors' wives, or lay leaders, I asked him, "What is the most important single quality of a father?" Without equivocation, he said, "Consistency." He went on to explain: "A boy doesn't have a chance if he never knows what to count on from his dad and mom. In fact, a boy has a better chance to grow up a good Christian if his dad is angry all the time than if he's moody and the son doesn't know what to expect." This is an oversimplification, but the emphasis is right. Paul said, "Fathers, provoke not your children to anger, lest they be discouraged" (Col. 3:21). Even discipline should be administered to guide and to rehabilitate, rather than to justify the short patience of a parent. David said, "Thy rod and thy staff they comfort me."

3. Rivalry and discord are reduced among children when the home becomes a bulwark of love and security. "Better is a dry morsel, and quietness therewith, than an house full of sacrifices with strife" (Prov. 17:1). Efficiency in financial planning, kitchen operation, housecleaning, and even child care is secondary to the need for building a bulwark of love and security within the home. Only the parents can provide this.

Reacting to Jealousy

Effective people are always subject to jealousy from others. When you stand to your feet, or lift your voice, or distinguish yourself from the crowd, you are going to experience the wrath of someone's jealousy. Sermons are often preached against jealousy in ourselves, but seldom, if ever, do we hear a sermon on how to react to jealousy when you are the victim.

There are at least three reasons why people may be jealous of you:

1. People may be jealous of your successes. This is especially true if others feel in competition with you. It is almost positively true if you have been in open competition and excelled.

2. People may be jealous of your goodness. Persons who have allowed themselves to be victimized by sinful habits tend to be jealous of those who have not. The writer of Ecclesiastes outlined the words of goodness and then concluded "that for this a man is envied of his neighbour." The Psalmist observed, "They envied Moses also in the camp, and Aaron the saint of the Lord" (Ps. 106:16). If the behavior of saints cannot escape the jaundiced interpretation of jealous observers, neither can present-day Christians who try to live the life of holiness.

3. People may be jealous of your possessions or

what they imagine your possessions to be. The farming successes of Isaac plus his possessions in flocks and herds were more than the jealous Philistines could handle. "The Philistines envied" him.

What can be done about it? What attitudes can a Christian acquire to deal effectively with himself when he is the victim of jealousy? Here are four suggestions:

1. Pray for grace to rise above petty jealousy. The sinful attitudes of others need not tarnish you if you can be ten feet tall on the inside. Striking back only adds heat to the fire and raises your own temperature. Sir Thomas Brown said, "Let age, not envy, wrinkle thy cheeks; be content to be envied, but envy not."

2. Pray for grace to understand the cause of this jealousy. You may have triggered this jealousy in others by flaunting your achievements and successes in front of people who already feel inadequate and anxious. Understanding the cause of the fire will not reduce the heat of the flame, but it may help in the strategy for extinguishing the blaze.

3. Pray for grace to be patient while God works out the problem. Joseph was sold into slavery by his jealous brothers, lied about by a vicious woman, and forgotten by fellow prisoners whom he helped. Later as prime minister of Egypt he was confronted by some of those whose jealousy had been most destructive. To them he said, "As for you, ye thought evil against me; but God meant it unto good."

4. Pray for grace to forgive. It was the coalition of jealous priests and an anxious, uncertain Roman governor which nailed Jesus to the Cross. But the first words which Christ said on the Cross were a prayer, "Father, forgive them; for they know not what they do."

None of us needs to expect immunity from the jealousy of others. But we may expect the grace of God to make us equal to the challenge.

31

When Christians Are Sanctified

All Christians believe in some form of sanctification. Catholics hold that we are cleansed from sin in purgatory. Some good people believe we are saved from our sins and then grow into sanctification by a gradual process. Other good people believe we are saved and sanctified all at the same time. Many claim that we are sanctified at the time and article of death.

Dr. J. O. McClurkan, an early church leader in Nashville, once believed in the "death theory" of entire sanctification. When Mrs. McClurkan became very ill and believed her illness was a prelude to death, she called in her husband to pray with her for the experience of entire sanctification. God heard their prayers and did a double miracle. He sanctified Mrs. McClurkan and healed her at the same time. When the truth of the circumstances dawned on her, she said, "Daddy, what shall I do? You have always preached that I could be sanctified at the time of death and now the Lord has sanctified me and healed me at the same time. What shall I do?" His reply was forthright. "You keep right on testifying to the experience of entire sanctification, and I'll change my theology." He did just this. And his tabernacle became the holiness center from which the

Church of the Nazarene in that area and Trevecca Nazarene College came.

The New Testament makes a clear distinction between "having" the Holy Spirit and "being filled" with the Holy Spirit. As the disciples were gathered in the Upper Room on the first Easter, Jesus "breathed on them, and saith unto them, Receive ye the Holy Ghost" (John 20:22). But it was to these same men he "commanded . . . that they should not depart from Jerusalem, but wait for the promise of the Father, which, saith he, ye have heard of me. For John truly baptized with water; but ye shall be baptized with the Holy Ghost not many days hence" (Acts 1:4-5). Six times in the Acts of the Apostles was the Holy Spirit poured out on believers as a crisis in religious experience. Let the Scriptures speak for themselves on "when" a person is sanctified:

Acts, chapter 2: On the Day of Pentecost the Holy Ghost was poured out on the followers of Jesus who had obeyed His command to wait for the "promise of the Father."

Acts, chapter 4: Several thousand persons had become believers during the period after Pentecost. Peter and John, who had just come from a frightening experience with the Sanhedrin, gave a report to the "company" of believers, who then joined in a mighty, united prayer. "And when they had prayed, the place was shaken where they were assembled together; and they were all filled with the Holy Ghost, and they spake the word of God with boldness" (v. 31).

Acts, chapter 8: When Jerusalem heard that Samaria had experienced a great revival, they sent their two best preachers, Peter and John, "that they might receive the Holy Ghost: (for as yet he was fallen upon none of them:) . . . Then laid they their hands on them, and they received the Holy Ghost" (vv. 15-17).

Acts, chapter 9: Saul, who was converted on the

33

road to Damascus, was visited by the local pastor, who reported the Lord had sent him that Saul "mightest receive . . . sight, and be filled with the Holy Ghost" (v. 17).

Acts, chapter 10: This early chapter in Church history, which often is called the Gentile Pentecost, contains the story of the Holy Spirit coming on these early believers. "While Peter yet spake these words, the Holy Ghost fell on all them which heard the word" (v. 44).

Acts, chapter 19: The final outpouring of the Holy Spirit recorded in Acts was on the Christians at Ephesus. They reported to Paul that they had "not so much as heard whether there be any Holy Ghost" (v. 2). After that, they were baptized "in the name of the Lord Jesus. And when Paul had laid his hands upon them, the Holy Ghost came on them" (vv. 5-6).

It does appear that the experience of entire sanctification (or the baptism of the Holy Ghost) does come as a second definite work of grace wrought in the heart of the believer subsequent to regeneration.

What Sanctification Will Not Do

The words sanctify, sanctified, and sanctification are used 164 times in the Word of God. In the Old Testament "things" were sanctified. For instance, the seventh day was sanctified, the altar in the Temple was sanctified, and Mount Sinai was sanctified. In the New Testament these words took on new meaning. Christ spoke of His own sanctification and the sanctification of His followers (John 17).

The Scriptures teach that both salvation and sin

are twofold in nature. Salvation is not only the changing of the outward life to conform to Christian standards, but a change of nature by the power of God's grace. And as salvation is both inward and outward, so is sin. There are sinful acts to be forgiven; there is a sinful nature to be cleansed. Justification involves the forgiveness of sins committed; entire sanctification involves the cleansing of the nature of sin within us. Thus the power of sanctification is manifest in the Holy Spirit, who cleanses the mind of sin and imparts the mind of the Spirit, divine love. Men whose lives have been characterized by violent outbursts of uncontrolled temper suddenly have a new image. Persons who were self-oriented suddenly evidence emotional involvement with others. Rigid, unbending personalities suddenly take on the pliability and resilience of a lovable person. One of the "sons of thunder" becomes "the beloved disciple." A loud, unstable, impulsive Simon becomes the rock, Peter.

But sanctification is not a cure-all. This "treasure in earthen vessels" is still very much inhibited. Here are a few of the limitations:

1. Sanctification does not take away the freedom of man to choose. In spite of current philosophy and psychology, which tend to be deterministic about man's behavior, there is no evidence to indicate man does not have the power of choice. God endowed man with a free will. He may live either for God or against Him. He has the right to choose. Even sanctification does not destroy this God-given capacity. It is not likely, but it is possible, that a Christian who has been sanctified for years may set his will against God, break fellowship with Him, and go into willful sin. A Christian may still backslide even after he is sanctified.

2. Sanctification does not place a Christian beyond temptation. The types of temptation to which we are

susceptible change and evolve as we go through the life cycle. But the potency of temptation is always there. Ananias and Sapphira, who probably were present on the Day of Pentecost, allowed themselves to be taken in by a deception of Satan which forfeited their status in grace and brought them immediate personal destruction.

3. Santification does not remove all the cultural prejudices which a Christian has been taught. Peter was sanctified in the second chapter of Acts, but he did not get rid of this prejudice against another race until the tenth chapter when God sent him to minister to Cornelius, an Italian, a Gentile. "You've got to be taught to be afraid of people whose eyes are oddly made. You've got to be carefully taught." Cleansing the heart of sin does not seem to alter automatically the wrong thought processes which have been learned from childhood. The sanctified Christian is still human and therefore subject to the mistakes of the head.

4. Sanctification does not make a Christian mature. Maturity comes from growth after sanctification. The saintly qualities of Paul while he wrote his prison letters, and of the aged and saintly John, are not the qualities they immediately possessed at Pentecost. They were cleansed and filled with the presence of Christ in Damascus and in the Upper Room so they might mature through the experiences of the years.

5. Being sanctified does not make Christians uniform. It might be wonderful if everyone saw things alike, but not nearly so interesting. No two people are alike on earth, even when each has been filled with the power of the Holy Spirit. There are differences of cultural background, educational achievement, emotional temperament, and strength of personality, to mention a few. Even if we all agree on a given proposition, it probably is for different reasons.

The Pastor and His Wife as Counselors

Whether they like it or not, the pastor and his wife are counselors. People constantly ask for help—on the phone, at the altar, in the corridor of the church, on the street, at the parsonage, and in the church office They want individual help from their pastors and pastors' wives, and have a right to expect it. In a United States Office of Education survey the results indicated that nearly half of all persons who come to the attention of doctors, clinics, and hospitals dealing with personal problems first sought help from their ministers, Whether or not the pastor and his wife are prepared to give help depends on their own spiritual resources, temperament, and understanding of human and carnal nature. But ready or not, the people come!

In warmhearted, holiness churches people seek help not only from the pastor and his wife, but also from Sunday school teachers, youth workers, lay leaders who have evidenced spiritual depth, and others. Studies indicate that people will seek help from authorized church personnel who provide time to see them, from persons who have seemingly handled their own problems effectively, from people who will take time to listen and respond, and from persons who will not think less of others for hearing their problems.

Since a liberal wing of Protestantism has substituted

counseling and psychology for the theology of the Cross, many good holiness people have resisted anything which looks like a dependency upon human understanding instead of the grace of God. And rightly so! But this does not change the fact that the pastor and his wife, plus all other leaders in the local church, already are involved in an obligation to help people who come to them with their personal problems.

The problems young people bring for help generally are drawn from the following list; (1) Choosing a vocation; (2) Social problems, including dating, courtship, and marriage; (3) Educational problems, such as choice of a college or curriculum and the effective ways to study; (4) Personal problems involving attitudes, conduct, and relationships with their family and with other young people.

There was a day when most of the counseling was done with young, single people. But now the pressures on and within the home are too great to be ignored. Couples who have lived together for years suddenly find they don't know how to talk out their problems with each other anymore. Money making and management, chronic fatigue, boredom, alcohol, personal relationships, and involvement with relatives are a few of the kinds of problems married people want to talk about.

All this suggests that the Christian worker or parent should be the last to resist personal involvement through counseling as a way to help people. As God works through the dentist's drill to alleviate the problems of tooth decay, and through the doctor with his surgical tools and medicines to eradicate pain, so God also works through His own saved and sanctified people in helping folks who are caught in an inner and outer web of circumstances which result in stress. The altar in the church is the place where sinners may be forgiven and believers sanctified, but the parsonage living room, the church office, the Sunday school classroom, the church corridor, or the street corner may be the place where God also chooses to work.

Last, Christian counselors know God not only works through the understanding and empathy of the worker who is reinforced by the presence of the Holy Spirit, but God also works simultaneously in the mind of the person who has come for help. Seemingly, God has endowed man with the capacity to gain insight into his own problem if he can articulate that problem in a non-judgmental atmosphere. "But we have this treasure in earthen vessels, that the excellency of the power may be of God, and not of us" (II Cor. 4:7).

The Sin God Can't Forgive

Adultery, lying, stealing, blasphemy, murder—all these sins and more will God forgive. But there is one sin He cannot: *the unconfessed sin.*

The concept of sin is not only theologically sound; it is psychologically sound. Billy Graham met with a conference of psychiatrists at Yale University. After two days they agreed they were both trying to deal with the problem of sin and guilt, but by different means. Dr. Hobart Mowrer, research professor of psychology at the University of Illinois and past president of the American Psychological Association, not only expresses grave doubt about the reliability of psychotherapy (and this after thirty years in the profession), but he has written that "emotionally ill persons are typically guilty persons, i.e., persons with *real* guilt rather than mere guilt *feelings*." He goes on to say, "Perhaps the *next* half century will be well spent if we do nothing more than learn how, once again, to make use of meaningful and effective restitution as a regular and expected concomitant of confession" (*The Crisis in Psychiatry and Religion*).

There are at least four observations to be made on unconfessed sin:

1. Hidden sin is a major roadblock to the flow of love and joy in a life. Trying to live happily over the top of unconfessed sin is like trying to force water through a pipe which is clogged with rotting debris. Even though some water passes the blockage, it is tainted in color and smell and its flow is slower and smaller than might normally be expected. When the filth and rottenness are cleaned out, the water flows full and pure. So it is with unconfessed sin. Even the finest moments in life are tainted by hidden sin. Life becomes small and choked when there's sin hidden away in the soul, unconfessed.

Even her roommates were disturbed over the strange irritability, sudden bursts of crying, and lack of concentration of their friend who normally was a radiant person and a good student. After three visits with the pastor, the girl suddenly exploded into tears and blurted out: "I can't keep it any longer. You won't tell anyone, will you?" After a confession of sin which would have stopped the flow of joy in any girl, prayer was made for forgiveness which only God can give. And it is not really strange that other problems seemed to melt away when sin was confessed to God and forgiven by Him.

2. Unconfessed sin cannot be lived down. Some people go on pretending to be happy, thinking sin will go away if it is ignored. The Portland *Oregonian* newspaper carried a little squib about a man who travelled

two thousand miles across the country to visit a former Oregon employer and confess the theft of a few dollars in tools more than a decade ago. The employer had forgotten the incident and the matter was not recorded in the company books. No court could have made a decision regarding the man's guilt. The reporter had mixed feelings of amusement and admiration. But to the man involved this was serious business. For ten years he had been beaten about by unconfessed sin which would not go away until it was made right. That same news note could be written with different names and addresses hundreds of times over. Why? Sin cannot be worn out by ignoring it. It can be overcome only through confession and forgiveness.

3. Confession always involves willingness to make restitution. Confession is more than awareness of sin. Confession involves forgiveness, and forgiveness cannot be forced against an unwillingness to make amends. Not every wrong can be made right, but many can. The most rewarding words in any vocabulary are, "I am sorry." The most self-satisfying words are, "I was wrong."

4. Only God can forgive. There is no efficacy in the psychiatrist's couch or the psychologist's counseling room —nor even in the pastor's study for that matter. Forgiveness is divine; it comes from God alone. The psychiatrist may help uncover the hidden rudiments of sin. the psychologist may help the person to articulate his problem in a nonjudgmental atmosphere. The pastor may lead the person to seek the grace of God. But only God forgives sin, and His power is limited to sins which are confessed.

Putting Away Childish Things

The most amazing computer in the world is the human brain. A scientist recently said that man might possibly make a computer which could do the things a human brain can do, but a building larger than the Empire State Building would be needed to house it, and at least one-half the power from Niagara Falls would be needed to run it.

But in a small volume of space God has given man a mind which can recall scenes and events many years old, in fascinating detail in either color or black and white. Man can receive, sort, assimilate, organize, analyze, and even project information with amazing speed and accuracy, all with his built-in computer, the human brain.

One of the tasks the brain deals with early in life is an answer to the basic question, what kind of person am I? Through the years of growing up the child continually collects information on this question, feeding it into his mind. By the time the child is in his middle teens he has a fairly clear picture of what kind of person he is, based on the feedback he gets from the persons who have been meaningful to him. His attitudes and behavior, then, tend to be consistent with this picture.

But what happens to this child and his mental picture? When a boy becomes a man does the child die or fade away? Where does this boy go when suddenly the grown man appears? The answer is simple. The little boy is still on the inside. Like the layers of an onion, maturity has covered the child with the sophistication of an adult body, an educated mind, legal responsibilities, and other adult facades. But the inner child of the past is still there, often dominating adult behavior. And it is tragic that many adults ineffectively face life with the emotions, decision-making processes, and articulation of a thirteen-to-fifteen-year-old. They never have put away being children. The Apostle Paul must have understood this when he wrote to a disturbed church, "When I was a child I talked as a child; I understood as a child; I reasoned as a child; but when I became a man I put away childish things" I Cor. 13:11, Wesley's version).

Childish thinking is completely self-centered. The child is the very center of his world. He cares little for the feelings, conveniences, or desires of others. So long as his needs and wishes are catered to, other people can worry for themselves. But when Paul became a mature person he took self from the throne and made Christ the center of his life.

Children can be brutal when they talk. They snarl, deflate, and mutilate each other's egos. When they have run out of accusations, they continue their baiting by making and reciting nasty little rhymes about each other. Adults are more sophisticated in doing the same thing, which they call "honest criticism." The person who backbites, criticizes, and finds fault is doing nothing more than raising a sign which says, I feel inferior to this person and I am going to trim him to my size, so I can feel more comfortable. Paul said he put away this kind of talking when he became a man.

Paul also put away childish understanding. This means he quit jumping at conclusions, stopped making decisions on impulse, ceased being guided by emotional prejudice, and stopped other evidences of juvenile thought processes. He realized his view of others was like a man in dark glasses. He was not qualified to judge. And since he could not qualify to make value judgments on everything and everybody, he filled his mind with faith, optimism, and love, which were far more abiding than childish wisdom.

An Apology to Teen-agers

There is a tendency among adults to look down on the new generation. The little girl turned to the little boy as they waited in the back seat of the family car for their father, who was coming through the rain from the house to drive them to school. "Now he'll tell us how far he had to walk to school when he was a boy and how much easier we have it then he did at our age."

These feelings of superiority by each older generation are not really harmful. They can be amusing. But with this current generation there has been a tendency to make the teen-agers the scapegoat for all the sins of the culture. In many instances this is unfair. In fact there are times we owe an apology to teen-agers.

Some need to apologize for failure to understand the nature of teen-agers. Observe a boy thirteen and compare him with a young man of nineteen. In this dramatic span his body and personality have undergone a complete overhaul. Even his voice has changed. He has learned to live with new emotions and feelings about sex which leave him confused and uncertain. This is the period when a child becomes an adult, a time when great amounts of reassurance and understanding are needed. But for many teens this is a period when they feel most rejected and misunderstood.

Then we need to apologize to teen-agers when we judge them all by a few. The police captain in our city said that fewer than 3 percent of the teen-agers in town come in contact with the law, and more than 80 percent of this small group live in one area fifteen blocks square. A very small but very loud minority on the campus near our church held boisterous noon meetings to affirm their right to experience literary "filth." This made spectacular front-page news, which was construed by many adults as just more evidence that the entire generation of college and high school students is rotten. It is no more right to judge all teen-agers by a few than it is to judge all doctors, preachers, or policemen by the small proportion of charlatans among them.

We also owe an apology to teen-agers when we fail to understand their basic problems. First is the problem of a vocation. In a day of specialization and complicated technology the untrained don't have a chance. The mediocre will settle for dull jobs while the prepared become the achievers. This vocational preparation is a major teen-age problem.

Second is the matter of a life's companion. There were more girls eighteen years old married last year than those of any other age. In one large university more than one of every four students is married. This decision which parents may wish to be postponed is now a major teen consideration.

And third, it is during teen years that final decisions often are made concerning religion. In Michigan State University a study of the problems of sophomores indicated their greatest concern was at the level of belief and understanding about God. We may already owe an apology to the Church of tomorrow if we are raising them on food and fun while we ignore the needs they feel most.

The Influence of a Good Woman

Back of most great men has been the influence of a good woman. Augustine might never have been heard of had it not been for the persistent prayers of his mother, Monica. The dynamic influence of Susanna Wesley on her son John caused later historians to say, "John Wesley first became a Methodist at his mother's knee." Even his enemies called Abraham Lincoln "Honest Abe." Lincoln's first ideas of ethics were learned from his mother, Nancy Hanks, who died when Lincoln was nine years old. Likewise the influence of Ida Eisenhower cannot be separated from the successes of her sons, particularly Dwight, who became the thirty-fourth president of the United States. Here is evidence of the power of the Christian home and a Christian mother.

Dwight Eisenhower came from a devout family. His parents were River Brethren. As loyal members of this religious group, they moved from Pennsylvania to Kansas because "Pennsylvania became too worldly." Ida's husband worked in a creamery. Then he opened a small business, which failed. Humiliated by "going broke," Mr. Eisenhower took the family to Texas. Here Dwight, the future president of the United States, was born. Time, which is a healer of many wounds, worked in favor of Ida Eisenhower and her husband, who eventually moved back to Abilene, Kansas.

There were six Eisenhower brothers who joined in a regular family Sabbath custom—preparing the entire

Sunday dinner and washing the dishes. There are many stories about these dinners and the problems the boys stirred up. One time they were making a pie. When the dough was rolled into a firm ball, they could not resist the temptation for an informal game of catch. Because of pitching and catching errors, Mother Eisenhower later recalled the crust was dark in spots, although the pie was good.

Besides attending church regularly, all of the boys read the Bible through each year and committed passages to memory. Prayer was a very important part of family scheduling. It is because of this early training of Ida Eisenhower that it seemed a natural thing for her son, upon his inauguration as president of the United States, to matter-of-factly say, before delivering his address: "I want you to join me in prayer."

Times have changed, but the factors which buttressed the Eisenhower home in the early days are sound principles for the Christian home now:

1. The effective Christian home is a bulwark of love and security. A $40,000 house with two cars in the garage and a fund to guarantee college education for the children does not become necessarily a home. It takes "a heap o' livin' in a house t' make it home." It takes love and understanding to give a child security.

2. The effective Christian home is an organized working unit, each person respecting the rights, seniority, and feelings of the others. Not every home needs a Sunday dinner prepared by the children, but every home does need children who are prepared to make their contribution to the ongoing of the family unit. Most modern children receive too much and participate too little.

3. The effective Christian home must refine the technique of family communications. Family prayers are not only spiritually needful but psychologically sound.

47

The dinner table needs to be a forum, not an arena. And the dining room chairs need to be the place where family members share each other's burdens in prayer. Children stalk out from a family setting where they have not learned to talk out their problems.

4. The effective Christian family takes attendance and participation in church services and activities for granted. Families who do not attend church regularly are usually guilty of committing one or both of two sins: either they wait until Sunday morning to decide whether or not they will attend church, or they break the Sabbath day by staying up too late on Saturday night. In either case the results are the same and church becomes an irregular means of grace.

The Tragedy of Postmortem Kindness

Next to bread the greatest longing of the human heart is for kindness." Love "suffereth long, and is kind." "Be kindly affectioned one to another." These and other sayings from sacred and secular literature are reminders that kindness is our most lethal weapon against a blasé society. Kindness is like the air in a cushion (according to Durbanville's *Winsome Christianity*). There's really nothing to it, but it helps take the jolts out of life. But the tragedy about kindness is that many people who matter the most to us often are taken for granted until it is too late for our expressions of kindness to be meaningful. Consider these two Bible passages:

"Then took Mary a pound of ointment of spikenard, very costly, and anointed the feet of Jesus, and wiped his feet with her hair: and the house was filled with the odour of the ointment" (John 12:3).

"After this Joseph of Arimathaea, being a disciple of Jesus, but secretly for fear of the Jews, besought Pilate that he might take away the body of Jesus . . . And there came also Nicodemus . . . and brought a mixture of myrrh and aloes, about an hundred pound weight" (John 19:38-39).

These two scriptures are set in contrast. The first demonstrates the devotion of a loving heart which was expressed with one pound of expensive ointment while the Saviour was alive. The second passage tells about a rich man who used a hundred pounds of ointment to express his hidden feelings—but only *after* the Saviour had died on the Cross. Which was better, one pound of ointment used while Jesus was alive or a hundred after He died?

It is a real tragedy to keep the alabaster boxes of our love sealed until our friends and loved ones are gone. An expensive casket and a great array of flowers are useless to a mother or father who would have appreciated a letter or telephone call to brighten the gray days of their declining years. An expensive toy bought by a very busy father is no real compensation to a little boy who would rather have two hours of his dad's time on Saturday. A big, expensive wedding, bought with the double income of Mother and Dad, doesn't really make up for the hundred afternoons when a little girl came home from school to an empty house. A big farewell gift to a departing pastor is not the same as a spirit of continued kindness during the years he was spiritual leader of the church.

How may we overcome the tendency to postmortem kindness? Here are a few suggestions:

1. Begin being thoughtful today. Abraham Lincoln once said he had no trouble finding men who would give

their last drop of blood for their country, but he had difficulty finding men who would give the first drop. Kindness is only hard to start; it runs itself after the process is under way.

2. Incorporate kindness into your regular program of giving. Give your tithes, offerings, time, and energy, but don't forget your capacity for kindness. In some instances a word of kindness is worth more than money. After Saul of Tarsus was converted in Damascus, he returned eventually to Jerusalem to make contact with the Christians. Everyone was afraid of him except Barnabas who, was friendly to Saul. His show of kindness made it possible for Saul and Peter to spend two weeks together. Who can estimate this gift of kindness by Barnabas!

3. Accept graciousness as a standard in Christian living. Christians have several standards on which their Christianity is judged. There are doctrinal soundness, ethical living, personal religious experience, and church loyalty. These are important, all of them. So is graciousness.

Christian kindness is better than a great deal of religiosity, and it reads a lot better than most gospel tracts. Kindness is the indirect witness for Christ—the soft sell. But kindness may be the best means we have to prove the grace of God to our neighbors. They may ridicule churchgoing and standards of separation from the world, but no one can gainsay the graciousness of an act of Christian kindness which is done naturally.

Home on the Rocks

As an apprentice Carpenter, Jesus knew what He was talking about when He told the story about two houses—a story with which He closed the Sermon on the Mount.

Jesus implied that the two houses were alike except for their foundations. One was built on the rock and the other on sand. Jesus spelled out facts these Palestinians knew well. The rains fell with their springtime fury. Rivulets beginning in the highlands were torrents by the time they reached the plains. Creek beds, usually dry, suddenly overflowed. The Jordan River, hardly challenging most of the year, became a raging flood. Every house in the path of these streams was put to the test. Some houses stood and others fell.

Jesus not only knew about houses; He also knew about homes and the dynamics of living together. Therefore the lessons of this parable are found in their application to our homes and families.

1. First, Jesus knew that every family has its share of storms. The difference was not in the fury of the storm against the Palestinian houses but in the strength of their foundations. The home in which no one lifts his voice to express shock or resistance, or drops his countenance to register disappointment, or flashes fear through his eyes, or withdraws to deal with his own problems of petty jealousy is not only abnormal, but unrealistic.

Frayed nerves may trigger a crying spell. Fatigue

51

lowers the level of patience and reduces the capacity to rise above turmoil. Persistent confusion dilutes inner strength. No one knows this better than a tired mother who strives valiantly to fill her role as cook, taxi driver, tutor, cleaning woman, purchasing agent, laundress, and family psychologist, all the while trying to be an understanding wife to her husband and an effective worker in the church. The storms which blow against your house are related to your age and maturity, as well as that of your children. But be assured that every family in your church and among your friends has storms of some kind.

2. Jesus was saying that the most threatening storms in life beat against the foundations of the home. Problems which brew in the outside world of work, school, and even at church, can be handled adequately if the bulwark of love and security at home is firm. School psychologists know that children will bring the unsolved home problems into the classroom. Normally, the problems of school are not a threat to the child who feels secure at home.

3. Jesus was also saying that He is the Foundation of every home which stands against the storms of life. In the Sermon on the Mount, Jesus has a good bit to say about things in the home. He mentions such practical articles as salt, candles, and lampstands. But He also gives major consideration to love, adultery, and divorce. Salt in the food, candles on the table, and lampstands to decorate the rooms do not make the house a home. The house is not really a home until Christ becomes its Foundation. His presence assures attitudes of love and understanding among family members. His presence insures against the deterioration and breakdown of the home by such threats as adultery and divorce. "And the rain descended, and the floods came, and the winds blew, and beat upon that house; and it fell not: for it was founded upon a rock."

Wives and Husbands

Literal interpretation of isolated verses in the Bible has caused people to do many strange things. Handling poisonous snakes in the name of the Lord, practicing the holy kiss, insistence on Saturday as the true day of worship, abstinence from eating pork, and canceling insurance policies are a few examples.

Paul's admonition for women to submit themselves to their husbands as the head of the house has also suffered from overly literal interpretation. It reads: "Wives, submit yourselves unto your own husbands" (Eph. 5:22).

Men have used this verse as leverage to impose their own unreasonable demands on their wives. By their own interpretation men have made this verse give themselves arbitrary superiority. This scripture has been used by some in an unscriptural way to gain selfish purposes.

Whatever else Paul meant by this passage, he did not mean that husbands may arbitrarily command their wives to obey them without respect for their wives' own ideas and feelings. A more realistic translation says, "Women, *adapt* yourselves to your own husbands."

The challenge for women to adapt themselves makes sense to thoughtful husbands who strive for mutual respect in their marriage relationship.

What does it mean for wives to adapt themselves to their husbands?

1. First, a wife who adapts herself to her husband finds marvellous fulfillment in his achievements. One of the surest ways to bring stress into a marriage is for her to become a competitor with her husband. This applies to work, earning power, or any other area of married life. Of course, the opposite attitude is also devastating. The wife who withdraws from interest in her husband's work, fishing excursions, golf score, or new car is opening the door for her own private emotional problems, as well as added home stress. Wives should not become little nobodies without feelings and opinions. Certainly they can work and have careers. But even so, the happiest wives, generally, are those who have adapted themselves to the interests, goals, purposes, and general way of life of their husbands.

2. Second, the wife who adapts herself to her husband is usually the person who keeps open the channels of communication between them. Research in human nature has shifted rapidly in recent years from adult problems which result from abnormal childhood to adult problems which result from a lack of a meaningful relationship with another adult human being. This "meaningful relationship" is based on open channels of communication. This means defenseless conversation, emotional involvement, and the therapy of cooperative work and play. In the home, this "meaningful relationship" may sometimes involve physical touch and even creative silence.

3. Third, the wife who adapts herself to her husband gives and receives strength through him. It is the same old truth that great men are often made by strong, effective women. More than one husband who might have been ordinary has risen above the crowd because of the woman in his life. As a result of giving herself to her husband many a woman who has been otherwise uncertain and inadequate has found a new strength. This is the analogy Paul used; for as the Church receives

strength from its Head, who is Christ, there is another kind of strength women receive who adapt themselves effectively to their husbands. "For the husband is the head of the wife, even as Christ is the head of the church: and he is the saviour of the body" (Eph. 5:23).

The Discipline of Children

The Apostle Paul includes in his admonitions to the family some sound observations about children. "Children, obey your parents . . . for this is right." He underscores the importance of obedience by reminding the families in Ephesus that the first commandment with a promise is about long life to children who honor their fathers and mothers.

There is no more difficult function in the home than the discipline of children. It is further complicated by the fact that much whipping and otherwise striking of children by parents is done in wrath and not in love.

Spanking is often a safety valve for the parent's anger instead of a useful tool for rehabilitation.

Parents who justify striking children in anger on the grounds of needed discipline do not understand what James meant when he said, "The wrath of man worketh not the righteousness of God." This does not mean children should not be spanked. (I spanked my five-year-old this morning.) But it does mean that no discipline—improvement of character—is achieved by parental outbursts of anger which result in impulsive striking of children. Parents would wither if they knew what went on in the minds of children during a parental beating.

Paul also warned, "Fathers, provoke not your children to wrath: but bring them up in the nurture and admonition of the Lord." This indicates parents bear a responsibility in the conduct of their children, in prevention as well as cure. An adult can provoke a child to misbehave and then punish the child for his misconduct.

If a father embarrasses a boy in front of his friends, or picks at him until he explodes in a burst of anger, does the dad have a right to punish the child? Does a perfectionist mother have the right to punish a two-year-old for not sitting quietly through a long sermon? Can a child be punished for not doing beyond his physical and emotional capacity to do?

Discipline calls for great amounts of understanding. And the parent who whips or punishes most must have the most love. Children may develop a fear which causes them to perform like robots in response to parental commands. But discipline which brings a change of attitude in the child or further encourages his development toward responsibility must be done with understanding and love.

Parents may do well to remember that capital punishment has never been proved a deterrent to murder. The child who feels he is the object of wrath or the butt of punishment because of the parent's own embarrassment is only provoked to greater acts of disobedience and more rigid attitudes of resentment.

A closing prayer: "O God, our Father, meditation about family relationships causes our feelings of inadequacy to grow stronger. None of us has final answers. But teach us, O God, to be more adequate in our adaptations to one another in the family. Direct husbands in communicating fully the love they feel toward their wives and children. And show every child that it is right to be obedient. We pray this in the name of Christ, who also was a member of a family here on earth. Amen."

The Sin No One Talks About

Problems of attitude and behavior are faced frankly today by more people than ever before. Struggles with anger, resentment, and self-pity are admitted and discussed openly. But among these, jealousy is too often omitted. It is always deplored when observed in others, but few people can be honest enough to recognize and admit jealousy in themselves.

Margaret Blair Johnson in a report of her research on jealousy said, "During the last sixty years, popular magazines have carried fewer than sixty articles dealing with jealousy—and all but seven of them were mainly concerned with telling parents how to keep older children from being jealous of the new baby."

But jealousy is not reserved for children. Arnold Gesell, a great research psychologist, said, "Jealousy is not a transitory affair peculiar to infants, children, and youth. It persists into ald age . . . if not always as a conscious motive, nevertheless pervading little things and great, from the peanut stand to a continental railway system, from a sewing circle to the congress."

Christians are interested in jealousy because it is mentioned many times in the Bible as both an acceptable and an unacceptable motive. God said of himself, "I the Lord am a jealous God." The brothers of Joseph experienced jealousy of the most destructive type. "When his brethren saw that their father loved him more than

57

all his brethren, they hated him, and could not speak peaceably unto him" (Gen. 37:4).

Jealousy may be detected and exposed within ourselves by one or more of the three cloaks it often wears:

1. A person often acts disinterested when underneath he is jealous. The elder brother of the prodigal son is not the last man who has disguised his jealousy behind the mask of a strange and untimely disinterest. A man who was promoted to a very important responsibility received many congratulatory communications, but none from his own brother who was in the same profession. "I did not know until then," he said, "that my brother was jealous of my achievements." It takes more grace to appreciate a man's successes than it does to comfort him in his failures.

2. Jealousy often expresses itself by depreciating the person or things which make us jealous. Examples of this are the urge to throw mud on a white suit, the tendency to puncture another's balloon, the satisfaction in seeing another's pride crushed. Children fight with their fists; adults use words. A jealous person may even use the flimsy disguise of "humor" to strike a humiliating blow. Others join the company of disciples who wanted Jesus to call down fire out of heaven to burn up the village which had withheld its hospitality. Angry, jealous people are still burning up those who make them feel inadequate.

3. Then, jealousy can show itself in outright acts of destruction. The plot against Joseph has been a pattern for many other jealous brethren. Only a few entertain thoughts of actual murder. Most will settle for the progressive assassination of a man's character. By asking questions which throw a shadow on a man's integrity they imply they could tell much more if their sense of ethics would permit. But all the time they are driven by an inner fire of jealousy instead of the pure desire for righteousness.

Does jealousy have a cure? Need human nature be victimized by this parasite? A problem which has its roots in the moral nature of man cannot be solved alone by suggestions about good mental health. Jealousy, like other sins of the nature, is subject only to the grace of God. Solomon said, "Envy [is] the rottenness of the bones." Paul said, "Ye are yet carnal: for whereas there is among you envying and strife . . ." James said, "But if ye have bitter envying and strife in your hearts, glory not, and lie not." By the cleansing grace of God there is a more excellent way: "Charity [love] suffereth long, and is kind; charity [love] envieth not."

The Lily and the Self-centered Life

Jesus held a Galilean lily in his hand one day and said to His followers: "Consider the lilies of the field . . . even Solomon in all his glory was not arrayed like one of these" (Matt. 6:28-29). If *even Solomon* was the most universally accepted symbol of grandeur and beauty against which a lily should be compared, then what kind of man was he?

1. Solomon was the first king of Israel who was the son of a king. He was born into the purple and soft raiment of a palace. The glory of the empire he built was a reflection of his own lavish tastes. Crowned king when he scarcely was out of his teens, Solomon coveted a grandeur that none could rival. He strove to

raise himself to a pinnacle of unapproachable isolation. And he did!

2. To begin with, Solomon developed a worldwide system of commerce. He imported horses from Egypt at bargain prices. Spices and gold were brought to him in caravans as tribute from the kings of Arabia. He developed a commercial navy which operated at great profit in both the Indian Ocean and the Mediterranean. He opened trade routes to the Tigris and Euphrates river valleys in the east and to Tyre and the Phoenician ports in the west and north. He built store-cities along the routes to protect his vast resources. His wealth became so vast he stopped counting it in silver and used only gold; "silver was not any thing accounted of" in the days of Solomon. Even his drinking vessels were of gold, all the silver ones being replaced.

3. But Solomon was no miser. He spent his money on incredible building projects and on lavish living. His ideas would stagger the imagination of modern builders and city planners. First he built the great Temple in Jerusalem. Fir and cedar trees from Lebanon were lashed together in rafts and sent by sea to Joppa and from there conveyed overland to Jerusalem. Solomon sent 30,000 people from Israel to Lebanon to work in the harvest of trees. Another 70,000 porters carried the loads, while an additional 80,000 persons worked in the stone quarries. The vast preparation of stone and wood was completed in three years. It is almost unbelievable that the timbers and stones were precut with such accuracy that "neither hammer nor axe nor any tool of iron was heard in the house." The walls were lined within and without with cedar and then overlaid with gold along with the ceiling and walls.

4. It took 7 years to build the Temple, but it took 13 years to build his house. The palace contained among other things a great judgment hall 150 feet long and 75

feet wide. In this hall was Solomon's throne made of ivory and overlaid with gold. His feet rested on a footstool of pure gold. The 6 steps leading up to the throne were ornamented with carved lions, also of ivory and gold. The walls were decorated with 500 gold shields, worn on special occasions by the palace guard. Around the palace he had vineyards, orchard, gardens, and trees which were watered by pools which sent through them a thousand murmuring streams. Forty thousand stalls were built for the horses.

5. When Solomon rode out into his gardens he was dressed in gleaming white. He was surrounded by guards, distinguished for their height, riding on prancing Arabian horses. The guards carried bows in their hands while mantles of purple were thrown across their armour. Their long hair, which was curled in clusters over their shoulders, was powdered every day with gold dust, which glittered in the sunlight.

If ever there was one human being who had wrung from life all it had to offer in fame, fortune, and personal comforts, he was Solomon. But in the decadent decline of his last years Solomon saw that everything he had made for himself was mocking him. He was a success in the self-centered life. More than any other person Solomon demonstrated the vexation of what "I" can do for "me."

There are not many potentates, not many rich, only a few who are well-to-do. But the attitude of Solomon is all about us because it is the nature of unredeemed man to see how much "I" can do for "me." Whether the income is $50.00 per week or $50,000.00 per year, the result is the same if life is centered in self. Maybe this is what Jesus meant when He said, "Consider the lilies of the field, how they grow; they toil not, neither do they spin: and yet I say unto you, That Solomon in all his glory was not arrayed like one of these."

Men Who Love Their Wives

Paul was not a married man, or at least not at the time he wrote his letter to the Ephesians, but he had sound advice on the love men should have for their wives. In one paragraph (5:25-31) he gives four sound directives:

1. First, men need to love their wives with a complete involvement even to the point of self-sacrifice. "Love your wives, even as Christ also loved the church, and gave himself for it." What greater joy does a man have than to give himself fully to the woman he loves and who loves him? No work is too hard and no sacrifice is too great for the man who loves and is loved.

2. A husband's love for his wife has a purifying effect. "Husbands, love your wives, even as Christ also loved the church . . . that he might sanctify it . . . that he might present it to himself . . . not having spot, or wrinkle, or any such thing; but that it should be holy and without blemish."

There is no better way for a man to bring out the best in his wife than to love her—and let her know it! A woman does not respond to commands or threats or aloofness. But she does respond with better attitudes and even improved physical health when she accepts the sincere love of her husband. This kind of love has a purifying, beautifying effect.

3. Third, this kind of love expresses itself in tender care and concern. "So ought men to love their wives

as their own bodies. He that loveth his wife loveth himself. For no man ever yet hated his own flesh; but nourisheth and cherisheth it, even as the Lord the church." A man caters to his own body. He provides it with rest, exercise, and relaxation. He keeps his own body comfortable, clean, and as free from trouble as possible.

Paul says this same care and concern is shown in the love of a man for his wife. She too may be catered to, protected, given opportunity for rest and personal relaxation. She needs private time of her own. When she suffers, he is concerned. When she faces a problem, he is moved to care.

This is not the role of a weak husband who simply responds to the whims of his wife like a servant to his master. It is the implementation of a deep, growing conjugal love based on mutual respect and understanding which develops between couples who possess the love of Christ.

4. Finally, a man proves his love for his bride by separating himself emotionally from his mother and father to become one with his wife: "For this cause shall a man leave his father and mother, and shall be joined unto his wife, and they two shall be one flesh."

Some men make inadequate husbands because they go through years of married life without ever leaving father or mother, emotionally. (Sometimes parents resist letting their children "leave.") Even in their own homes these men behave as though mother and or father were there giving the directions. The apron strings have never been cut. They are not adequate marriage partners because they have never gotten away from the maternal domination of their boyhood homes.

When wives adapt themselves to their husbands and husbands love their wives, the home is on its way to another great step toward abundant living.

What Money Can't Buy

Someone has said that reading the Book of Ecclesiastes is like holding on to both poles of a battery; it is a succession of shocks. The writer took for his text, "Vanity of vanities; all is vanity!" (Eccles. 1:2). He observed that history was going in circles and "there is no new thing under the sun" (Eccles. 1:9). In spite of the opulent Oriental splendor in which he lived, the king said, "I hated life," (Eccles. 2:17). When he compared the ways of men and beasts he saw no difference: "As the one dieth, so dieth the other; they have all one breath; so that a man hath no preeminence above a beast; for all is vanity" (Eccles. 3:19). "The race is not to the swift, nor the battle to the strong, neither bread to the wise, nor riches to men of understanding; for time and chance happeneth to them all" (Eccles. 9:11). But with shocking impact he goes on to say, "A feast is made for laughter, and wine maketh merry: but money answereth all things" (Eccles. 10:19).

This idea that money answers all problems is both the most popular idea among people today and the most erroneous. The entire culture is based on the idea that money is the first thing to try in seeking solutions. And in a sense this is true. Money will buy the basic needs of the body. And beyond this it will supply according to its abundance the comfortable, secure way of life. But that is all! In a world which is roughly divided between the *haves* and the *have-nots,* money can become mighty important. Money has been described as the sixth sense without which the other five don't count. To a member of the Mod Generation, money won't buy happiness but it will make the down payment on a car to use in searching for it. But it still is a fact that, beyond the basic physical needs and standard comforts, money doesn't buy the things that really count.

1. Money won't buy self-discipline. In fact money tends to work against the discipline needed for achieving excellence. Among professional athletes, the best competitors are "hungry." Scholars, ministers, writers, politicians, and others who work for excellence in one way or another have long been fearful of the temptations money brings. Only the rare person can rise above the abundance of money to live in a self-disciplined way which results in excellence.

2. Money can't buy encouragement. Although receiving money as a reward or payment may be an encouragement, money cannot be spent to buy reassurance, uplift, and encouragement. Department stores and private shops do not stock encouragement and would laugh at the person who tried to buy it. Encouragement comes from God, generally through people who are His intermediaries.

3. Money won't even buy good health. A considerable amount of money may be spent on doctors whose "practice" may be helpful. But the physicians themselves are the first to refrain from promising good health regardless of the fee.

4. Last, money can't buy peace of mind. Clinics, hospitals, and the "worry book" sections of bookstores are filled with people trying to pay for peace. It can't be done! Peace comes from forgiveness and cleansing, from the radical change of attitudes, from the acquisition of a new set of values. In all his letters, Paul begins and ends with the words "grace and peace." They go together, for it is God's grace (and not money) which brings peace to troubled minds.

The Psychology of Christmas Giving

When first voted by Congress, the income tax was declared unconstitutional by the Supreme Court. Not easily discouraged, backers of the idea sought and got an amendment to the Constitution which cleared the way for the great American institution of income tax. At the beginning, a tax of 1 percent was made against an adjusted income of $20,000; this graduated up to 6 percent above the $200,000 level. Today this tax system touches every home. The income tax has done many things to the American scene in the last twenty-five years; not the least is the revolution it has caused in giving.

In the old days a man gave in response to an impulse to generosity. But today's donations are made on the basis of the accountant's tax projections. Big business does its giving through self-directed foundations which are statistically controlled in a manner to make an insurance actuary proud. Even the most committed Christians seem compelled to regulate their giving at a level declared "deductible" by the Internal Revenue Service.

Systematic church giving tied to the regulations of income tax deductions is tolerable and perhaps even necessary. But the psychology of it has entered into Christmas giving. The idea of giving Christmas presents comes from the act of adoration by the wise men who brought gold, frankincense, and myrrh to the Baby Jesus. Contrary to the psychology of much Christmas giving, this act by the Magi was unselfish, done with no thought of return or personal advantage.

Real giving is not truly honest unless it represents something of the giver. The gift is a projection of the self. When David prepared to make an offering to God, a friendly king offered to give him the place and the cattle for sacrifice free of charge. But David said: "I will surely buy it of thee at a price: neither will I offer burnt offerings unto the Lord my God of that which doth cost me nothing" (II Sam. 24:24). Unless our Christmas presents represent something of ourselves in time, energy, planning, creativity, thoughtfulness, and even sacrifice, they are obligations expedited on the basis of duty.

Love, when it is expressed in word, deed, or gift, is almost always extravagant and often impractical. Mary broke a pound box of ointment for Jesus while Judas mumbled about the high cost of giving and the needs of the poor. Even the generosity of the wise men to the Baby Jesus would have scandalized the practical-minded innkeeper. Joseph's multicolored coat and the widow's mite are further examples of extravagant love.

Another quality of Christmas giving is emotional involvement. Jesus said the only kind of love to God and people which is acceptable involves the heart, soul, and strength. A Christmas present which involves the mind and heart indicates the giver has had personal joy in planning, choosing, financing, wrapping, and delivering the gift. It is a symbol of thoughtfulness. This explains the great personal joy a parent feels on receiving a handmade gift from a child. The commercial value of the gift may be nil but no mark can be set on its worth. The gifts we prize most are those which indicate the greatest amount of emotional involvement by the giver.

Finally, the greatest kind of gift has a spiritual quality. Jesus said: "If ye then, being evil, know how to give good gifts unto your children, how much more shall your Father which is in heaven give good things to them that ask him?" (Matt. 7:11) One little boy shocked his father into a period of heart searching when he asked for Christmas that his dad give two hours of time each Saturday for a year. The boy wanted more than things; he wanted his father. God's greatest Gift to us is His Son, the Supreme Gift we experience through the presence of the Holy Spirit.

How to Know You Are Saved

Attempting to restrict God's grace and forgiveness to a system, a list of rules, or a set of spiritual laws, is risky business. No two people come to Christ in the same way. Saul of Tarsus encountered Christ through an experience that involved a vision, a voice, and temporary blindness. The Ethiopian eunuch found Christ through Philip's helpful explanations of Isaiah. The Philippian jailor came to believe on the Lord Jesus Christ during the aftermath of an earthquake. Even great church leaders have not been stereotyped: Augustine found Christ while reading his Bible in the garden; Luther was converted through library study; Wesley's heart was "strangely warmed" by the reading of a commentary. None of these were saved in a Sunday night evangelistic service. Nonetheless, there are certain guideposts which can help direct a person into confident, saving faith, based on the authority of God's Word:

1. The road to salvation begins when a sinner realizes his lostness and his need of forgiveness. There

is no other starting point. Saying, "I'm as good as everybody else," however true, is not the attitude for obtaining God's grace. Paul knew this when he wrote, "By one man sin entered into the world, and death by sin; and so death passed upon all men, for that all have sinned" (Rom. 5:12). The weeping prophet, Jeremiah, wrote, "The heart is deceitful above all things, and desperately wicked" (Jer. 17:9).

2. The first guidepost is passed on the road to heaven when the sinner realizes his own acts of righteousness cannot save him. Turning over a new leaf only affords opportunity to smudge another clean page in the book of life. No person deserves salvation. It cannot be exchanged for any quantity of acts of goodness. Isaiah knew the futility of seeking righteousness through willpower: "All our righteousnesses are as filthy rags; and we all do fade as a leaf; and our iniquities, like the wind, have taken us away" (Isa. 64:6). "A man is not justified by the works of the law," wrote Paul to the Galatians who sought salvation through the law, "for by works of the law shall no flesh be justified" (Gal. 2:16). And to the Ephesians he said that grace "is the gift of God: not of works, lest any man should boast" (Eph. 2:8-9). To find salvation, self-righteousness has to go.

3. The next major guidepost is passed when the sinner realizes that salvation comes only through Jesus Christ. Salvation is not contained in the altar, the preacher, the doctrine, or even the Church. Salvation comes through the indwelling presence of the person of Christ. Peter, whose life was radically changed by Christ, knew this: "For Christ also hath suffered for sins, the just for the unjust, that he might bring us to God" (I Pet. 3:12). Timothy, the faithful student of Paul, said, "This is a faithful saying, and worthy of all acceptation, that Christ Jesus came into the world to save sinners" (I Tim. 1:15). "And the Lord," said

Isaiah, "hath laid on him the iniquity of us all" (Isa. 53:6).

4. The final two guideposts toward knowing you are saved are repentance and faith. "Except ye repent," said Jesus, "ye shall all likewise perish" (Luke 13:3). "For by grace are ye saved through faith; and that not of yourselves" (Eph. 2:8). Salvation is not an intellectual understanding nor an act of worship. It is the accepting of a Person, Jesus Christ, as the risen Lord and Master of life.

The mind and heart are prepared to receive Christ as the sinner realizes (a) his lostness and need of forgiveness, (b) the futility of self-help and self-righteousness, (c) the fact that salvation comes only through Jesus Christ, and finally (d) that he must repent with godly sorrow for all sinful acts and attitudes. But all these steps are futile unless the final step is taken to accept Jesus Christ by faith for forgiveness and His transforming presence.

How to Know You Are Sanctified

Some Christians who have no problem accepting God's grace for salvation and forgiveness seem to struggle over the spiritual step between the new birth and entire sanctification. The reason most often given is, "I can't understand it." Neither can one "understand" electricity or aerodynamics, but this does not discredit the use of electrical conveniences or jet transportation. The fact that one cannot explain the new birth does not hinder him from experiencing the transforming power of salvation. Then why should lack of intellectual understanding be a roadblock to the infilling of the Holy Spirit? Really, the Scriptures are plain as to the way to be sanctified.

1. To begin with, the seeking Christian must realize that Christ died on Calvary for the sanctification of believers as well as the forgiveness of sinners. The New Testament Scriptures document this fact: "Wherefore Jesus also, that he might sanctify the people with his own blood, suffered without the gate" (Heb. 13:12). "By the which will we are sanctified through the offering of the body of Jesus Christ once for all" (Heb. 10:10). ". . . to them that are sanctified in Christ Jesus" (I Cor. 1:2).

2. The seeking Christian may be assured that Christ commanded the sanctification of His disciples. Christ seems to have been a quiet, soft-spoken Man who more often taught than preached. Not often is the word "command" used to describe the manner of Jesus. But He did give an explicit command to the disciples on the coming of the Holy Spirit. "And, being assembled together with them, commanded them that they should not depart from Jerusalem, but wait for the promise of the Father, which, saith he, ye have heard of me. For John truly baptized with water; but ye shall be baptized with the Holy Ghost not many days hence" (Acts 1:4-5). On another occasion He spoke directly to them: "Tarry ye in the city of Jerusalem, until ye be endued with power from on high" (Luke 24:49).

3. God's Word indicates sanctification is necessary for victorious living. In His great prayer for the disciples whom Jesus was soon to leave, He said, "I pray not that thou shouldest take them out of the world, but that thou shouldest keep them from the evil. Sanctify them through thy truth: thy word is truth" (John 17:

71

15, 17). When the disciples asked Jesus about the restoration of Israel to the old status quo of pre-Roman days, He answered, "It is not for you to know . . . but ye shall receive power, after that the Holy Ghost is come upon you" (Acts 1:7-8). God's method of victorious living is to provide inner strength rather than ameleriate outward circumstances.

4. The next big move by the Christian seeking entire sanctification is a new, deep, moving experience of consecration and soul searching. This must have been what happened among the disciples who waited together for ten days in the Upper Room in spiritual preparation for the coming of the Holy Spirit on Pentecost. This same need for consecrated Christians is underscored in the writings of Paul. Addressing those Romans whom he called "brethren, by the mercies of God," Paul urged them to present their "bodies a living sacrifice, holy, acceptable unto God . . . that ye may prove what is that good, and acceptable, and perfect, will of God" (Rom. 12:1-2). In another place in the same letter he said, "Yield yourselves unto God" (Rom. 6:13). To another church he wrote, "For this is the will of God, even your sanctification . . . that every one of you should know how to possess his vessel in sanctification and honour" (I Thess. 4:3-4).

5. And finally, the Christian who seeks God for entire sanctification must believe Him for the experience. The Holy Spirit comes in His fullness by faith only. "And God, which knoweth the hearts, bare them witness, giving them the Holy Ghost . . . purifying their hearts by faith" (Acts 15:8-9). In his testimony before King Agrippa, Paul again indicated that sanctification is by faith, just as the new birth is. He said his own commission from Christ was to the Gentiles, that he might "turn them from darkness to light . . . that they may receive forgiveness of sins, and inheritance among them which are sanctified by faith that is in me" (Acts 26:18).

Sins of Busy People

If the Church becomes cold and useless, it will not be because the members decide suddenly to throw aside their Christian responsibilities and to denounce their faith. When the congregation gives evidence of worldliness, it is at least partly because the members got too busy in legitimate demands on their time to nurture their Christian faith. In fact the most universal sins among Christian adults and their families are the sins of busy people. There are three major ones: (1) sins of omission, (2) sins of excusing ourselves, and (3) sins of broken fellowship.

1. One of the first steps away from Christian power and usefulness toward spiritual anemia and atrophy are *the sins of omission.* Failing to assume one's share of responsibility in the church or omitting attendance in regularly scheduled services of the church, for example, are not considered by most people to be as offensive in the sight of God as the blacker and more easily recognized sins of conduct. But are sins of omission less damaging than sins of commission? James said, "To him that knoweth to do good, and doeth it not, to him it is sin" (Jas. 4:17). When Jesus described the realities of the judgment (Matt. 25:41-46) He said to those guilty of the sins of omission, "Depart from me, ye cursed, into everlasting fire . . . for I was an hungred, and ye gave me no meat: I was thirsty, and ye gave me no drink: I was a stranger, and ye took me not in . . . Inasmuch as ye did it not to one of the least of these, ye did it not to me." The most frightening factor about the sins of omission are the sub-

tlety with which they are "practiced" and the lightness of people's attitudes toward them.

2. The second kind of sins of busy people is the *manufacturing of excuses* to justify their actions (or inaction). One does not need a high IQ to be able to rationalize the strangest kinds of behavior. Once a decision to do a certain thing is made, even on an emotional instead of a factual basis, the unconscious signal is given to the brain to come up with justifiable reasons for the action. But these "reasons" are often nothing more than feeble excuses. When G. Campbell Morgan was a boy, he failed to complete an assignment of homework one night because of company which came to the home of his parents. In lieu of the finished work he took an orthodox excuse signed by his mother to the teacher the next morning. It was received with a nod, and little Campbell Morgan went to his desk. At the end of the day when class was dismissed, he started to leave with the rest of the children. Stopping him dead in his tracks, the stern master said, "And what about your assignment of last night, young man?" "Oh, I brought you an excuse for that, Sir," the boy replied. "Right you are," continued the teacher, accenting his voice with his loudness. "An excuse is just what it was, but the work is still to be done." The boy sat down again and stayed at his desk until the previous night's assignment was finished. He learned one of the great lessons of life that day, that even the best excuse is no substitute for unfinished work.

3. The third of the sins of busy people is *the sin of broken fellowship.* "Demas hath forsaken me," wrote Paul, "having loved this present world" (II Tim. 4:10). When well-meaning people have become too busy to nurture their faith, and have rationalized their sins of omission with inadequate excuses, then the final result is a life lived apart from the Church and out of fellowship with Christ. And it all started innocently enough—just the result of being busy people!

74

What Is Secularism?

From church administrators, pastors, theologians, Sunday school teachers, and leaders in religious education, the one word used to describe today's culture is "secularism."

Present-day secularism shows itself in many faces: (1) *The secularism of the compartmentalized life.* An individual may be devoutly religious in one aspect of life, but at the same time effectively lock out God from other areas of living. (2) *The secularism of the practical atheists.* These are the people who live as if God did not exist. These people turn their backs on the Bible and the Church. They make their decisions and conduct their business and personal lives without taking God into account. (3) *The secularism of the Christian humanists.* These often are pleasant, gracious people who accept many of the by-products of the Christian faith such as honesty, morality, and service to one's fellowman, but reject a doctrinal Christianity.

But the disturbing thing about secularism in this day is the serious inroads it has made in the Church. There are at least four kinds of secularists in most congregations: (1) The church member who confesses faith in Christ and the doctrine of the Church but holds to the world's sense of values. (2) The nominal Christian who restricts his religion to a limited number of devotional acts. (3) The member to whom the Church is merely a business enterprise without personal involvement in the lives of others. (4) The person who tries to manipulate God for his own purposes.

But regardless of the faces secularism shows or the ways it masquerades in the Church, it has some definite identifying marks wherever it may be found—even in your own heart:

1. The secular man's basic tendency is to magnify the importance and self-sufficiency of man. Man, not God, has become the chief actor in the drama of moral progress.

2. The secularist believes that whatever gets results is good. Man's needs can be met through prayer; therefore pray. Church attendance makes man better; so go to church. Bible study will improve the personality; therefore join a Bible study group. Try tithing because it is the key to success in money management. Religion brings peace of mind, so turn to religion. All of these things are true in degree, but the essential element lacking in the practice of these ideas is God himself.

3. The secularist has a very light view of sin. Whereas the Bible pictures sin as being so terrible that only the death of Christ on the Cross can atone for it, the secularist will think of it as a matter of no great consequence. His means for overcoming "sin" are primarily social action, education, and a war on poverty.

4. The secularist will hold to a relative standard instead of an absolute moral code. If a thing is legal or widely practiced, it is right in the mind of the secularist. To him the drunkard becomes the man of distinction and lust is the natural expression of human nature.

5. The good life is equated with material abundance. Madison Avenue perpetuates the feeling that all needs can be met with things.

6. The secularist believes in redemption by science. He so understands and controls the forces of nature that he sees no need of God. Man is but a cog in the whole evolutionary wheel.

The Old-fashioned Square

In David Reisman's book, *The Lonely Crowd,* the American population is divided into three groups on the basis of their process for making decisions. (*a*) There are "tradition-directed" people who do whatever they do because this is the way it has always been done. The suggestion of change is discomforting. (*b*) Then there are the "inner-directed" people. They operate by an inner gyroscope, live with a central purpose, and have clear-cut direction. Their behavior is predictable because they have the same set of values wherever they are. These are the people who have made America. (*c*) And the third is the newly emerging group called "other-directed." They mostly are concerned about what others think. Their convictions are not deep, if at all. Acceptance is more meaningful to them than achievement. The problem is this: Any man who is "inner-directed" is considered by "other-directed" people as a square. The man with convictions is a real square in the sight of the man who has none. The teen-ager who stands up to be counted is a real square in the eyes of another teen-ager who melts away into the acceptance of the crowd.

The writer of the first psalm described a man who refused to go along with the crowd as a person who "walketh not in the counsel of the ungodly." Further, this old-fashioned square refused to waste his time in meaningless chatter and small talk with those whose highest good was to test the feelings of others; he "standeth not in the way of sinners." Finally this ancient man who was "inner-directed" did not even afford the luxury of being a religious bigot who thought himself superior to other people; he "sitteth not in the seat of the scornful." In addition, the first psalm suggests four additional characteristics of the old-fashioned square:

1. First, the old-fashioned square was a man of blessed happiness: "Blessed is the man" (Ps. 1:1). There is nothing wrong in seeking happiness but most people go about it in the wrong way. Will Rogers once wrote about a druggist who often was asked if he ever took days off for a good time. He said, "No, but I have sold lots of aspirin to people who have." Happiness does not come by seeking it. It is a serendipity; it comes by indirection as the result of something else. Useful people with a sense of self-esteem usually are happy. Human understanding fosters happiness. Living to reach goals tends to produce happiness. But regardless of the route, happiness always comes by indirection; it is not the primary goal.

2. Second, this ancient square meditated twice a day. Really, now, how square can you get? People think meditation is for elderly people who have nothing else to do, for a few saints, and for preachers who meditate as a part of their profession. Surely no young couple raising a family, paying off a mortgage, and fighting their way up the ladder of life will find help in daily meditation! But this ancient square who was blessedly happy found meditation helpful enough to involve himself in periods of quiet reflection twice a day. "In his law doth he meditate day and night" (Ps. 1:2).

3. Third, this old-fashioned square became like a tree planted near the water (Ps. 1:3). The man who is like a tree is stable in all seasons. His leaf does not wither under the sun because of his hidden source of

78

strength. His fruit bears regularly. In the Bible, a good man has been compared to salt, a city set on a hill, and to a lamp in the room, but there is no better metaphor to describe a real man than the tree planted near water.

4. Finally, the old-fashioned square, known by the Psalmist three thousand years ago, was an effective man; "Whatsoever he doeth shall prosper" (Ps. 1:3). Note that the man himself is not necessarily prosperous. But what he does prospers. Anything to which he gives his time and energy is productive. So, to be a square is not the worst thing in the world. It can be the best way to live.

Holiness in the Home

The Church does not lack for an adequate doctrine of holiness. And certainly the doctrine of the Holy Spirit is well represented in the hymnbook. The various holiness denominations stand as a tribute to the continuing work of the Holy Spirit in organized religion. But the real test of the doctrine of entire sanctification is not in the theology, the hymnbook, or in denominational statistics. It is found in the home. This is why Paul wrote the Ephesian Christians as families, "Be not drunk with wine . . . but be filled with the Spirit . . . submitting adjusting yourselves one to another" (Eph. 5:18-21). There are three major problems which frustrate the adequate work of the Holy Spirit in the home.

1. The "normal" home is not the same as the "ideal." A young couple facing marriage talk and dream about the home they will establish. This dream home

will be devoid of all the ills that were present in the homes in which they were raised. It will be a haven of joy and love and peace—a sort of perpetual honeymoon. In time the couple settles down to the practical problems of building a home and a life together. When the first sharp disagreement on ideas arises, the entire foundation of their relationship is threatened. They have made the mistake of expecting the "ideal" in life to be "normal." Homes do not operate on the level of the "ideal." Each person in the household is a separate distinct individual with his own set of fears, joys, ambitions, problems, and crystallized techniques for handling them. The Holy Spirit helps Christians adapt to one another effectively, but there is no such thing as the "ideal" family where everything runs so smoothly that the adults and children never have clashes which erupt in cross words with each other.

2. A main function of the home is to provide a place where members of the family may "let their hair down," or press the safety valve to let off tensions which have been building up during the day at work and at school. If the relationships in the home are so fragile that some tension-releasing act or behavior cannot be absorbed within the family, then the structure is faulty. The home is one place where family members may express themselves without restraint because the family know and understand each other in love.

Dedicated Christians as well as all members of the human race are made up of mind, soul, and body. Tensions develop in the mind and body and must be relieved or serious mental and physical complications result. It is the Holy Spirit who teaches Christians in families how to relieve tensions in the home without hurt to themselves or others. It is the Holy Spirit who teaches the Christian that he is a soul with a mind and a body which cannot be ignored.

3. Although living close together over long periods

of time can be exasperating, it can also be very rewarding. One of the men on Admiral Byrd's first expedition wrote about the problems of a small group of men living close together in a hut during the long months of the Arctic winter's night. They learned each other's idiosyncrasies, how a fellow took off his shoes, cleared his throat, and told old jokes. The very closeness of their relationship brought them to the brink of despair and madness. In turn each man would brave the numbing cold and possible death to go out into the Arctic night, just to be alone, away from the others. In later years the bonds of friendship thus established were lasting and fulfilling, but at the time, the inescapable closeness in the crowded quarters made them irritable and mutinous. Does not the same thing happen in families? Have you ever tried a cross-country trip of several thousand miles with three young children in the back seat?

These problems of give-and-take in the home, the need for a place to let off steam, and the necessity of living close together in small quarters, make the work of the Holy Spirit all the more important in the home. His presence in the home and within each member of the family helps us in the unending process of "adjusting one to another in the fear of God."

Money Is More Important
Than You Think

When Ernie Pyle, the famous reporter of battles in Europe and the South Pacific during World War II, was a cub reporter, he wrote a newspaper story about a certain man who had died leaving "a huge fortune of $15,000." When the editor chided him, saying a $15,000 inheritance was not "huge," Ernie Pyle said, "It all depends on who is doing the inheriting." True, to some people $15,000 is a fortune; to others it is a year's salary; to some it is a house; to others it is only the down payment on one.

Money is always relevant. When a new level of riches is reached, one is never fully satisfied. A new and higher level of wealth suddenly seems needful and the process of achieving starts all over. This is why the Bible says, "When goods increase, they are increased that eat them: and what good is there to the owners thereof, saving the beholding of them with their eyes?" (Eccles. 5:11).

This same writer concludes his discussion on money with one final, undebatable observation: "As he came forth of his mother's womb, naked shall he return . . . and shall take nothing of his labour, which he may carry away in his hand" (Eccles. 5:15). This idea, universally accepted, has been reduced to an old cliché, "You can't take it with you." And since money cannot be taken beyond the grave, it is all the more important what is done with it here. Money may be more important than you think!

Money is more important than you think if attitudes toward it are neurotic. A neurotic attitude, or fear, or reaction, is one that is exaggerated beyond the importance it deserves. A neurotic person may be afraid of sounds nobody else hears. A neurotic, unrealistic attitude toward money is expressed among some people in unwarranted caution and among others in a complete lack of control in money management and planning. One person spends fifty cents on gas to save ten cents on a grocery item "on sale" across town. Another person driven by emotional buying is obligated to monthly payments greater than his income. In either case, money is threatening his life. To the parsimonious man, money restricts the fulfillment of life; and to the spender, money becomes the occasion for turmoil, strife, and family disorganization. An accurate study of the financial situation and the development of a realistic set of attitudes toward both earning and spending are needed by all.

John Wesley recognized money as being about the best single index of holiness as a way of life. He preached his famous sermon on "The Use of Money" twenty-two times and then had it printed for wider distribution. In it he gave this formula: (1) *Make all the money you can.* Within the limits of hurting oneself or his neighbor, Wesley urged his people to make money. (2) *Save all the money you can.* Beyond the demands of prudent family living Wesley believed all other money should be set aside. (3) *Give away all the money you can.* The practice of the first two steps without the third leads to spiritual decay. Wesley gave away more than $90,000 in his lifetime and died with only enough money to care for his burial. He intended that his life and his money should run out at the same time.

If this formula of earning, saving, and giving is to be taken seriously, then every Christian needs to protect his estate after he is gone. It is a man's responsibility to see that the residue of his life's labor is continuing to be used as he would want it after he is gone. Maybe that is what the preacher meant when he said, "There is an evil which I have seen under the sun, and it is common among men: A man to whom God hath given riches, wealth, and honour, so that he wanteth nothing for his soul of all that he desireth, yet God giveth him not power to eat thereof, but a stranger eateth it: this is vanity, and it is an evil disease" (Eccles. 6:1-2).

The Status of Women

Women have much to be thankful for because of Christianity. In fact the New Testament writings on the family cannot be understood without knowing the place of women in the society of that time. Among the Hebrews a woman had no legal rights. She was the sole possession of her husband. The orthodox Jewish man prayed every morning thanking God that he was not "a Gentile, a slave, or a woman."

The interpretation of the Jewish law on divorce indicates the helplessness of women. The original statement on divorce is in Deut. 24:1, "When a man hath taken a wife, and married her, and it come to pass that she find no favour in his eyes, because he hath found some uncleanness in her: then let him write her a bill of divorcement . . . and send her out of his house."

Obviously the accurate use of this law depended on the interpretation of the little phrase *some uncleanness*. The stricter rabbis held that *some uncleanness* meant adultery. But the popular majority of rabbis were liberal in the widest possible way in their interpretation. Here are some of the things they said a man might use as a cause for divorcing his wife:

—if she spoiled his dinner with too much salt.

—if she spoke disrespectfully of her husband's parents.

—if she walked in public with her head uncovered.

—if she was troublesome or quarrelsome.

The narrative of Jesus and the woman at the well indicates she had been married to five different men, and the man with whom she was living was not her husband. Such were the marriage conditions in Palestine.

This was possible because the process of divorce was disastrously easy. In the presence of a rabbi and two witnesses a man could hand his wife a statement which said: "Let this be from me thy writ of divorce and letter of dismissal and letter of liberation that thou mayest marry whatsoever man thou wilt." If it were properly signed, the divorce was final. There was no testimony, no appeal, and no settlement except a man had to return his wife's original dowry.

Among the Greeks and Romans matters were even worse. For the Greeks, divorce was nothing but caprice. Among the Romans it was sport. Roman women numbered the years by the names of their husbands. Jerome declares it is true that in Rome there was a woman married to her twenty-third husband and she was his twenty-first wife.

When the New Testament Church began, the marriage bond was almost meaningless and the home was at a point of disintegration. It was against this background that Paul made three startling admonitions to the Christian familes among the Ephesians:

1. "Wives, submit yourselves unto your own husbands . . . for the husband is the head of the wife, even as Christ is the head of the church" (Eph. 5: 22-23).

2. "Husbands, love your wives, even as Christ also loved the church, and gave himself for it" (Eph. 5: 25).

3. "Children, obey your parents . . . for this is right" (Eph. 6: 1).

These ideas were not held by the people on the streets in Ephesus. Paul's challenge was revolutionary. What Paul did was to call men and women to a new fidelity, a new companionship, a new purity, and a new fellowship in marriage and the home.

The Miracle of Divine Healing

Man has always been concerned about his health. Every normal person wants to be healthy and every abnormal person is likely to be unduly concerned over his physical well-being. In the Bible the subjects of health and healing are mentioned too often to be ignored or written off as unimportant. The writings of all the Early Church fathers give evidence that healing did not cease with the death of the apostles. Today, spiritual healing is practiced by many groups. There are the healing cults such as Christian Science; the Roman Catholics, who maintain a number of healing centers such as Lourdes in France; the professional "faith healers" who advertise their purposes and powers widely; and some Protestant churches whose attitude toward divine healing ranges from skeptical acceptance to firmness of conviction.

There are five principles which lead to a better understanding of divine healing as known and practiced today:

1. Healing is a relative term. Every disease leaves some kinds of "scars" on the body tissue or psychological makeup, or both. Healing of the most radical and dramatic type is only partial, for death does eventually come.

2. All healing of every kind comes from God. This is true whether the cure comes through the surgeon's

scalpel, the magic of penicillin, the patient, dynamic listening of a psychiatrist, or through intercessory prayer. God works in many ways His wonders to perform. In fact, all these means are used in healing. In divine healing, faith, prayer, and the laying on of hands supplement rather than take the place of medical care.

3. "Divine healing" is not to be confused with "faith healing." Faith healing has more reference to faith in a dynamic healer than it does in the deep spiritual faith Jesus meant when He said, "Thy faith hath made thee whole" (Mark 5:34). People who emphasize healing are in danger of placing more emphasis on the healing than on the great theme of salvation. God is not a tool to be manipulated to gain human health.

4. For the Christian the matter of supreme importance is not bodily health but right relationship with God. One may be a profound Christian and yet suffer horribly. Being a Christian enables one to triumph over suffering through the all-sufficient grace of God (II Corinthians 12). An overemphasis on health may, and often does, lead to an overemphasis on self.

5. With the "gift of healing" sometimes goes the tendency to pride and self-righteousness because of an assumed closeness to God. Even in reporting the spectacular there may be the emphasis that others would have these miracles if they too had this special closeness to God. The less wise are prone to blame failure to heal on the lack of faith within the patient.

With some understanding of the place and meaning of divine healing there is need to understand the methods of the Bible in healing. There are three: (1) *The laying on of hands.* Paul advised Timothy on his methods (I Tim. 4:14 and II Tim. 1:6). Jesus touched the eyes of the blind men (Matt. 20:34); He touched the leper (Mark 1:41), Peter's mother-in-law (Matt. 8:15), and took the hand of the child (Luke 4:54). (2) *The anoint-*

ing with oil (Jas. 5:15-16). (3) *The prayer of faith* "Prayer changes things" (see Mark 9:29). Faith can remove mountains (Matt. 21:21). "Perfect love casteth out fear" (I John 4:18). These are the promises of God to those who come to Him in faith for healing.

Time Is How You Use It

Time is an abstraction. It cannot be seen, touched, or heard; and yet it exists. Mechanical schemes have been developed for measuring time but even these are not absolute. Clocks are on the desk and calendars on the wall but these measurements of time are in one dimension only. Who, for instance, can say how long a man has lived? Some people live a great deal in a short time while others only exist biologically for an allotted number of years. Methuselah lived for a long time, measured in a straight line, but his accomplishments are nil. On the other hand, his father, Enoch, whose years were only half as many, lived a life that had depth and height and width which this world could not contain, and only heaven could complete.

There is a skill in learning to do the right thing at the right time. "A wise man's heart discerneth both time and judgment" (Eccles. 8:5). The man who said that also wrote, "To every thing there is a season, and a time to every purpose under the heaven: a time to be born . . . to die . . . to plant . . . to pluck up . . . to kill . . . to heal . . . to weep . . . to laugh . . . to get . . . to lose . . . to keep silence . . . to speak; to love . . . to hate" (Eccles. 3:1-8).

John Wesley taught his early Methodists three principles about time and the way to use it:

1. Unprofitable or harmful talk is a misuse of time. If all conversations suddenly had deleted from them all the inconsequential and gossipy talk, there would be lots of unaccustomed silence on the party line and across the coffee cup. Wesley became so concerned about the misuse of good time for bad talk that he and Charles and eleven other preachers signed the following covenant:

"It is agreed by those who names are underwritten—

"(1) That we will not listen, or willingly inquire after any ill concerning each other.

"(2) That if we do hear any ill of each other, we will not be forward to believe it.

"(3) That, as soon as possible, we will communicate what we hear by speaking or writing to the person concerned.

"(4) That, until we have done this, we will not write or speak a syllable of it to any other person whatever.

"(5) That neither will we mention it after we have done this to any other person.

"(6) That we will not make any exception to any of these rules, unless we think ourselves absolutely obliged in conscience so to do."

2. Wesley urged early Methodists to correct improper uses of the Lord's Day. Dr. James B. Chapman in his pamphlet on *The Stewardship of Time,* said that a Christian "does not need special leadings to know what to do with one day in seven." The fourth commandment says, "Remember the sabbath day, to keep it holy." The Sabbath is kept in two ways: (*a*) refraining from secular activities, and (*b*) by maintaining a positive regard for this day as a holy day instead of a holiday. Some people break the Sabbath by their behavior and by keeping late hours before the Sabbath dawns. Saturday night activities should never be allowed to ruin Sunday morning effectiveness.

3. Wesley insisted that recreational diversions which offered no contribution to Christian growth or gravitated toward evil associations were a waste of good time. "He giveth us all things to enjoy so we enjoy them to his glory. But I say, avoid all that pleasure which in any way hinders you from enjoying Him." There is no small amount of room for contention concerning personal judgments on recreation. But in this day when labor is talking about a thirty-hour week and drudgery is being eliminated through useful gadgets, it is important for Christians to consider seriously their use of time.

The Shook-up Generation

One of the big problems of this "great society" is to find out what to do with the younger generation. This problem is perennial but especially acute in those years which follow a great war or other major social upheaval.

1. The generation of young people who went to high school and college during "the Roaring Twenties" —themselves the product of a great war—were described by Ernest Hemingway, Gertrude Stein, and F. Scott Fitzgerald as "the lost generation."

2. Following World War II there was a breed of teens and young adults which were referred to in England as "the angry young man," and in this country as "the beat generation." A newspaper reporter in San Francisco, where these young people tended to gather in the Northbeach section, referred to them as "beatniks" and the name has stuck ever since. The beatnik has

rejected every authority figure including the preacher, the teacher, and the policeman. The beatnik carried existentialism to its ludicrous conclusion. In his anger, frustration, and futility he has expressed his outlook on life in one sentence: "Get out of my road and leave me alone to live exactly as I want without the interference of outside authority or past standards of goodness." The beatnik is not only the captain of his own soul but the jury and the supreme court.

3. However, the beatnik is a relic of the past. His own system of values has become so widely accepted, we now have the "mod generation" with their far-out fashions and style of life. The spirit of revolt among today's younger generation is so widely accepted that their rebellion is now used as an advertising gimmick to sell Dodge cars. The essence of rebellion is now available in their own perfume bottles. What odor, pray tell, is appropriate to rebellion?

4. But one of the best descriptions of today's young people is given in the title of a book by the Pulitzer Prize-winning journalist Harrison Salisbury. He calls this "The Shook-up Generation." And he says they are shook-up because their parents are shook-up and they are being raised in shook-up homes.

A wise old king who lived nearly three thousand years ago spoke to the shook-up generation of his day who saw everything as vexation and vanity. He gave these young adults three suggestions which might be called "the three R's" for the shook-up generation:

First, "*Rejoice*, O young man, in thy youth . . . God will bring thee into judgment" (Eccles. 11:9). A free translation of this verse might read, "Take full advantage of your youth, for God will call you into judgment on how you used these precious years." Youth is the time for (*a*) educational preparation and (*b*) vocational choice. Any youth who does poorly in either of these areas stands in judgment on himself. For the Christian, every job is a calling just as much as the ministry. Therefore the choice of the right vocation and adequate preparation are the big challenge of the youthful years.

Second, "*Remove* sorrow from thy heart, and put away evil . . . for childhood and youth are vanity" (Eccles. 11:10). The teen years are not for sowing deeds which grow up to be sorrows. Evil is to be put away and not used for youthful experimentation. Youth is vanity—like a vapor—and slips away quickly. Therefore save a lifetime of sorrow by removing evil from youthful behavior.

Third, "*Remember* now thy Creator in the days of thy youth, while the evil days come not" (Eccles. 12: 1). God loves every teen-ager and has a plan for his life. Only sin prevents a person from fulfilling God's plan. Therefore, remember Him now, before evil days come. To remember Him is to repent; to repent is to turn to Him for forgiveness and for new directions.

You Can't Go Home Again

Anxiety, uncertainty, fear, and loneliness have motivated people of all stations in life to seek the security and tranquility of a former place or time. People in their adult years have tried in a thousand ways to turn back time, but every attempt is a failure. Everyone has to agree with Thomas Wolfe that "You can't go home again." He wrote, "You can't go back to your family, back home to your childhood, back home to romantic love . . . back home to places in the country . . . back home to the father you have lost . . . back home to someone who can ease the burden for you, back home to the old forms and systems of things which seemed everlasting but which are changing all the time."

In Thornton Wilder's story, "Our Town," Emily, who died and was buried on the hill, had her wish fulfilled to go back home and live again one day of her life. She chose her twelfth birthday. But even when she "turned back the clock" and went back home to go through one day of life exactly as lived, it was not as she remembered it. Even when the day had hardly begun, she cried out, "Take me back up the hill to my grave."

In his best-selling book, *Reminiscences,* General Douglas MacArthur told of his desire to go home again. But after describing in moving and bitter detail his failure in this attempt, he said, "I never went back again. I had learned one of the bitter lessons of life—never try to regain the past, the fire will have become ashes."

The children of Israel spent forty futile years wishing they could go back home to Egypt, which was a foreign land to begin with. Rising up in anger before Moses and Aaron, they threatened mutiny; "Were it not better for us to return to Egypt? And they said one to another, Let us make a captain, and let us return into Egypt" (Num. 14:3-4).

The ancient writer of Ecclesiastes understood this fact of life when he wrote, "Say not thou, What is the cause that the former times were better than these? for thou dost not inquire wisely concerning this" (Eccles. 7:10). It is human nature to think the old days were the really good days. And it is human nature to try our hand in unending ways to go back. Sociologists see in the present-day craving for antiques and Early American furniture an expression of such nostalgia. People try to go back through the lives of their children. Old clichés which are inadequate for new times are held on to like they were golden vessels. When things go wrong, the remedies of a previous era are brought out in an effort to effect a current cure. But the facts are, we can't go back, for at least three reasons:

1. You can't go home again *because the clock won't stand still.* With the passing of time there is the continual development within persons and within environments which effects inexorable change. This makes it impossible for things ever again to be just like they were before. People change; situations change; time marches on; the clock won't stop!

2. You can't go back because *this is the only day there is to live;* "This is the day which the Lord hath made; we will rejoice and be glad in it." This line from the Psalmist (and, incidentally, the favorite Bible verse of Lowell Thomas) is the only cure for looking back. Yesterday can be recalled only through memory. Tomorrow is unkown; it may never come. But this is the day the Lord has made for us to use; "rejoice and be glad in it."

3. You can't go back because *strength is not found in the past but in a Person.* The biggest reason for not trying to recapture the past is that strength and glory are not there; they are in the person of Jesus Christ. When the cumulative weight of life has become unbearable, don't turn back; He has come to give life and that more abundantly.

Predictions for the New Year

December is the time when columnists are writing their lists of the ten best or biggest or more important of whatever-it-is for this year. It also is the time when they are forecasting for the new year. CBS brings home its round-table specialists on international affairs who combine their knowledge to predict things to come. Sportswriters, congressional analysts, and market forecasters are among those who are predicting the shape of things for next year. Even the famous Jeanne Dixon, who foretold the death of President Kennedy, takes a look into her crystal ball for a clearer view of the future.

Really, predicting for the new year is not too difficult. Human nature has changed very little in the past six thousand years. On the basis of what happened last year and the year before, some things are fairly certain for the year ahead.

For most people, next year will not be a new, but another, year. They will live by the same prejudices, criticize the same people, and grumble over the same things. It takes courage to break out of old mental habits, and for the majority this is asking too much.

For most people, next year will be a time to make deeper ruts instead of new tracks. The same spiritual problems and the same overwhelming circumstances will be met in the same inept way next year. It takes spiritual power and confidence which goes deeper than the shallow commitment of most Christians in order to radiate the strength of God. Therefore they will deepen old ruts and avoid new tracks for another year.

For most people, next year will be another year for keeping busy, but not productive. Telephones will jingle, car wheels will spin, and lots of dust will be stirred. But in most instances the final cessation of the machinery will indicate the end of another time period, but not necessarily the achievement of meaningful goals. Personal productivity takes commitment, self-discipline, consecration, and hard work, days on end. This is asking a greater price than most folks will be willing to pay.

There is a way to make next year your year for overcoming; it can be the greatest year of your life:

1. Start the year with a period of self-analysis. "The unexamined life," according to one great man, "is not worth living." Set dates for regular, periodic checkups on attitudes, trends in behavior, and spiritual relationships. "Know thyself."

2. Set down on paper the specific goals which are meaningful for you. These may involve several areas of life, including mind and body, sacred and secular, home and business, personal and public.

3. Write out in detail the means to be followed in reaching the goals you have set. Give room for faith to work, for God to do the unexpected after you have exhausted your own resources in meeting these goals.

4. Follow up on yourself. Be your own taskmaster. Avoid rationalization of your failures to use self-discipline, faith, or work.

Live with Christ as Lord and Master of your life in a most practical way. A denominational Christian, a theological Christian, and an ethical Christian may be loyal to his church, understand the doctrine, live an impeccable life, and still not live as though Christ were really his Lord and Master. "I live; yet not I, but Christ liveth in me: and the life which I now live in the flesh I live by the faith of the Son of God" (Gal. 2:20).